PENGUIN BOOKS

THE FALL OF THE KINGDOM OF THE PUNJAB

Khushwant Singh was India's best-known writer and columnist. He was founder-editor of *Yojana* and editor of the *Illustrated Weekly of India*, the *National Herald* and *Hindustan Times*. He is the author of classics such as *Train to Pakistan*, *I Shall Not Hear the Nightingale* (retitled as *The Lost Victory*) and *Delhi*. His latest novel, *The Sunset Club*, written when he was ninety-five, was published by Penguin Books in 2010. His non-fiction includes the classic two-volume *A History of the Sikhs*, a number of translations and works on Sikh religion and culture, Delhi, nature, current affairs and Urdu poetry. His autobiography, *Truth, Love and a Little Malice*, was published by Penguin Books in 2002.

Khushwant Singh was a member of Parliament from 1980 to 1986. He was awarded the Padma Bhushan in 1974 but returned the decoration in 1984 in protest against the storming of the Golden Temple in Amritsar by the Indian Army. In 2007, he was awarded the Padma Vibhushan. Among the other awards he has received are the Punjab Ratan, the Sulabh International award for the most honest Indian of the year, and honorary doctorates from several universities. He passed away in 2014 at the age of ninety-nine.

The Fall *of the* Kingdom *of the* Punjab

KHUSHWANT SINGH

PENGUIN BOOKS

An imprint of Penguin Random House

PENGUIN BOOKS

USA | Canada | UK | Ireland | Australia
New Zealand | India | South Africa | China | Singapore

Penguin Books is part of the Penguin Random House group of companies whose addresses can be found at global.penguinrandomhouse.com

Published by Penguin Random House India Pvt. Ltd
4th Floor, Capital Tower 1, MG Road,
Gurugram 122 002, Haryana, India

Penguin Random House India

First published by Orient Longman Ltd 1962
Published in Viking by Penguin Books India 2014
Published in Penguin Books by Penguin Random House India 2017

10 9 8 7 6 5 4 3 2

ISBN 9780143440109

Typeset in Goudy Old Style by CyberMedia Services Ltd, Gurgaon
Printed at Manipal Technologies Limited, India

www.penguin.co.in

This book is dedicated to the memory of
Sardar Bahadur Sir Teja Singh Malik, CIE,
and his wife, Lady Raj Malik, who spent
the best part of their lives in the service
of their Gurus.

CONTENTS

Author's Note

This little book tells the story of the fall of the kingdom of the Punjab. It covers a period of ten years, from the death of Maharajah Ranjit Singh on the afternoon of 27th June 1839 to the morning of 14th March 1849 when the Punjabi armies laid down arms. Every character and incident mentioned in this narrative is based on contemporary historical records.

I wish to place on record my gratitude to the Rockefeller Foundation by whose munificence I was able to devote three years exclusively to research and the writing of Sikh history; this book is a by-product of that study. I would also like to acknowledge my indebtedness to M. L. Ahluwalia of the National Archives and my colleague and collaborator Miss Yvonne Le Rougetel who has assisted me in completing this work.

Authors Club
London S. W. 1.

Khushwant Singh

Chapter 1

Nightmare in Dreamland

'What does the red colour stand for?' asked Maharajah Ranjit Singh of an English cartographer who was showing him a map of Hindustan.

'Your Majesty,' replied the Englishman, 'red indicates the extent of British possessions in the country.'

The Maharajah scanned the map a little more carefully with his single eye and saw that the whole of India except the Punjab was painted red. He paused for a little while and then remarked to his courtiers: '*Ek roz sáb lal ho jaiga*—one day it will all be red.'

The anecdote about the map, like many other anecdotes about Ranjit Singh, was made up to illustrate the Maharajah's prophetic vision. But in the case of the British, one did not have to be a prophet to guess that they would extend their power to the utmost geographical limits of Hindustan—if possible, even beyond. In the forty years Ranjit Singh had been Maharajah of the Punjab, he had seen the English triumph over all the other princes of India: the Nawabs of Bengal and Oudh; the Rajputs, Rohillas, Jats and Gurkhas; they had even vanquished the most powerful of all Indian powers, the Marathas, from whom they wrested the capital city of Delhi, along with the Mughal Emperor. The only independent Indian Kingdom that remained was that of the Punjab.

The English made no secret of their designs to take the Punjab. In 1809, they had extended their frontier from the banks of the Jumna to the Sutlej, taking all the Sikh chiefs of Malwa under their protection. This was an aggressive extension of their earlier policy of considering the Jumna the western limit of their empire: it was also in flagrant disregard of the title established by Ranjit Singh who had thrice visited Malwa and been acclaimed by the Chiefs as the sovereign of all the Sikhs. Ranjit Singh had mustered his forces to resist this incursion, but then realised that he was not strong enough to fight the English and their Indian mercenaries. He had swallowed his pride and signed away Malwa.

The English provoked Ranjit Singh over and over again. Each time he talked of fighting them but lost his nerve and agreed to terms dictated by them. They blocked his progress southwards towards Sindh and the Arabian Sea. They began to meddle in the affairs of Afghanistan and cajoled Ranjit Singh into joining them in subverting the Barakzais and placing their own puppet, Shah Shuja, on the throne of Kabul. They had been audacious enough to suggest the posting of a British Resident in Lahore. This the Maharajah had firmly refused to accept. But he must have known that it was only a matter of time.

In his anxiety to ward off the British danger, Ranjit Singh had begun to modernise and increase his army. From 1822, a stream of European officers—French, Italian, Greek, Spanish, English and Eurasian—began to enter his service. All the major conquests had been made and there were neither new sources of revenue to pay the enormous salaries of the foreign officers and for modern weapons, nor new fields to conquer. Ranjit had on principle kept his troops in arrears of pay as it prevented desertions in time of action. After 1822, the shortage of money became chronic and it was only the iron discipline imposed by the Maharajah that prevented the troops from breaking out in open mutiny. The seeds of indiscipline had however been sown and Ranjit's successors had to reap the bitter harvest. Soldiers began to demand that their arrears be cleared forthwith and frequently refused to fight unless they were promised rewards and higher pay. They disobeyed their officers and used violence against those they did not like. European officers, of whom more than forty were on the payrolls of the Durbar, were the first to pull out. Even those who stayed did so because of the enormous salaries they drew (Ventura Rs. 2,500 p.m. plus a *jagir*; Avitabile Rs. 1,666 p.m. plus a *jagir)*. Their loyalties were not towards the Punjab State and they were more than willing to sell information to the British. Ranjit Singh had treated them as highly paid drill-sergeants and never reposed any faith in their professions of loyalty. Once when they had refused to contribute to a levy, the Maharajah had exploded: 'German, or English, all these European *haramzadas* (bastards) are alike.'

Ranjit Singh's army comprising both the *Ain* regulars trained by Europeans and the *Ghorchara* horsemen consisted of a little under 50,000 men with nearly 300 pieces of artillery of various calibre. There were, in addition, troops which the military fief-holders–*jagirdars*–had to provide. The army cost the State over one crore of rupees per year, i.e., more than one-third of the State's income. It was, however, the most powerful in Asia. To ensure their jobs, the European officers inculcated fear and hate of the English among the men (without themselves having any compunction of treating with English agents). It was not surprising that when the soldiery came to know how untrue to the Punjabi salt their Europeans had become, it developed acute xenophobia.

Ranjit Singh's greatest oversight was his failure to train any one of his sons to take his place. When he died on the evening of 27th June 1839, there was no one fit to step into his shoes and guide the destinies of the State. This applied not only to his sons but also to the rest of the favourites at Court whom he had raised from rustic obscurity to power, from modest means to wealth beyond their imagination.

Ranjit Singh left seven sons behind him. Since they were born of different women they had little fraternal affection for one another. Of these sons the eldest, Kharak Singh, who was thirty-seven years old, was his father's choice as successor. He was the least suited of the brothers, having inherited nothing from his illustrious sire except his plain looks and bad habits—particularly the love for laudanum and hard liquor. 'Besides being a block-head, he was a worse opium-eater than his father,' wrote the royal physician, Dr. Martin Honigberger. Kharak Singh had been brought up by servants who pandered to all his whims and was unable to develop initiative. He was easy-going but without any of the down-to-earth peasant simplicity which had endeared his father to the masses.

His indolence was, however, somewhat of a blessing as he was not unwillng to leave the tedium of administration to more willing hands.

Kharak Singh's son, Nao Nihal Singh, possessed the qualities his father lacked: ambition, drive and a pleasant personality. At the time of his grandfather's death, he was on the North-West Frontier, directing operations in the Afghan campaign on behalf of the Durbar. He was aware of his father's incompetence to manage the affairs of State or control the unscrupulous pack of courtiers who surrounded him.

An equally ambitious and affable claimant to the throne was Ranjit Singh's second son, Sher Singh. Sher Singh had made no secret of his aspirations and based his claim on being the son of Ranjit Singh's first wedded wife, Mehtab Kaur, and was altogether better suited to be Maharajah of the Punjab. Kharak Singh refuted Sher Singh's contentions and asserted that he (Kharak Singh) was the only legitimate son of his father: the others–Sher Singh, his twin brother Tara Singh, Kashmira Singh, Peshaura Singh, Multana Singh and the one-year-old Dalip Singh–were, according to Kharak Singh, of doubtful paternity.

In the absence of leadership from the Royal family, the Council of Ministers and the nobility at Court assumed greater importance. Since their primary interest was to enlarge their personal estates and privileges they found it politic to play one claimant to the throne against the other. Two factions emerged soon after the death of Ranjit Singh. The more influential were the three Dogra brothers,

Gulab Singh, Dhyan Singh and Suchet Singh, and Dhyan Singh's son Hira Singh, who had been a great favourite of the late Maharajah. Although the three brothers were not always in accord, one or another member of the family managed to be in effective power at Lahore and allowed his other kinsmen to set up an almost independent Dogra kindgom in the hills of Jammu and Kashmir.

Opposed to the Dogras were the Sikh nobility, particularly three families related to the Royal family, the Sandhawalias, Attariwalas and Majithias. The most influential were the Sandhawalias–Lehna Singh, Ajit Singh and Attar Singh who were also connected to Kharak Singh's wife, Chand Kaur. The Attariwala chiefs, at that time of little consequence, were Sham Singh, Chattar Singh and his sons, Sher Singh and Gulab Singh. The head of the Majithia family was the celebrated Lehna Singh, a scholarly person of somewhat retiring habits, and the young Ranjodh Singh, who was a military commander of note. Since the Dogras were Hindus, it was inevitable that the differences between them and the Sikh Sardars should assume a communal aspect. The one thing members of these factions had in common was the desire to reduce the crown to a mere cipher and become, like the Peshwas of the Marathas, the real rulers of the country. In doing so, few of them had any scruples about the methods they used to gain their ends: murder by poison or by hired assassins, betrayal of friends and relations after the most solemn vows, forging documents to discredit their rivals, and, worst of all, negotiating with the British who were then known to be planning the annexation of the Punjab.

There were amongst the coterie of self-seekers a small number of men who refused to align themselves with either faction and continued to serve the Durbar as faithfully and honestly as circumstances permitted. Outstanding among them were the Fakir brothers, notably the eldest, Azizuddin, who was adviser on foreign affairs, and a Kashmiri Brahmin, Dina Nath, who administered the departments of revenue and finance. Men like Azizuddin and Dina Nath were content to give advice whenever it was asked for but did not try to exert their influence on the violent men who had come into power.

Wrangling began while Ranjit Singh's body still lay on the floor awaiting cremation. The chief courtiers foregathered in the palace and agreed unanimously that 'no confidence could be placed in Koonwar Kharak Singh Bahadur and Koonwar Nao Nihal Singh Bahadur as regards the continuance of the estates in their possession.' The next day after the cremation they came to the palace and again desired their heir-apparent 'to console them (the noblemen) by a solemn oath on the Granth that the grants repectively conferred on them by the late Maharajah should be continued to them.' The newly-rich, upstart aristocracy of the Punjab thus made the continued enjoyment of privileges and property a condition for their loyalty to the State. It was not surprising that within a few days the main preoccupation of the Royal family and the nobility became the acquisition of more property and the throne was reduced to being a footstool on which the ambitious could place their feet to climb higher.

Maharajah Kharak Singh gave the necessary assurances and for some time assuaged the fears of the aristocracy. Relations between him and his brother Sher Singh continued to be tense for some time. Sher Singh had kept away from his dying father's bedside because he suspected that Kharak Singh would avail of the opportunity to seize him. His first instinct was to proceed to the hills and, if possible, take over the district and fort of Kangra. He gave up the plan when he heard of his father's death and instead repaired to his estates in Batala. He had it conveyed to the Durbar that he would not attend the obsequial ceremonies unless he was guaranteed immunity from arrest. Maharajah Kharak Singh gave his solemn pledge; Raja Suchet Singh and Jemadar Khushal Singh gave personal assurances that no harm would come to Sher Singh. The Prince came to Lahore and on the last day of the official mourning the *Punjab Akhbar* was able to report that there seemed to be great unanimity between all members of the Royal family. On 16th July 1839, Maharajah Kharak Singh invested his step-brother with the sonourous titles *Sri Wahguru ji ke piarey, Satguru ji ke Savarey, Ujjal didar, nirmal budh, akhri arshadi, aitzadi, Bhai Sher Singhji* (Beloved of God, perfected by the True Guru, radiant of face, of clear insight, the strength of our arms, the honoured one, our own brother, Sher Singh).

The unanimity in the Durbar did not last many days. Nao Nihal Singh decided to take over the affairs of the

State into his own hands. The *Punjab Akhbar* of 16th July 1839 (nineteen days after the death of Ranjit Singh) records: 'Nao Nihal Singh has made all the Sardars sign a document confirming Maharajah Kharak Singh's successor and his own *mukhtari* or ministership . . . he has issued orders to all Sardars at Lahore to defer the ceremony of *tilak* to his father till his return to Lahore, and to consider themselves responsible for the preservation of all the jewels, treasures and horses etc. left by the late Maharajah, of which he would take an account on his return. Raja Dhyan Singh was disconcerted on hearing of the *purwana*. The ceremony of *tilak* has been deferred till the month of October.' Some of the ministers lined up behind the Prince; others, including the Sandhawalias, backed Dhyan Singh Dogra. A few, like the Fakir brothers and Raja Dina Nath, kept aloof.

Dhyan Singh Dogra restrained the impetuous Nao Nihal from upsetting the carefully balanced apple-cart. He accepted the Prince's right to make major policy decisions and agreed to play the role of Chief Counsellor. At first, Maharajah Kharak Singh accepted this arrangement without demur. But later he came under the influence of one Chet Singh Bajwa, who was related to him through his wife and had been manager of his personal estates. Bajwa persuaded Kharak Singh to give up his dissolute ways, and take his duties as a monarch more seriously. He thus made Kharak Singh conscious of the usurpation of the royal prerogative. Tension grew between the Maharajah and Chet Singh Bajwa on one side and Prince Nao Nihal

Singh and Dhyan Singh Dogra on the other. Kharak Singh made a feeble effort to put his son and the Dogra Chief Minister in their places but it was obvious to all concerned that the initiative came from Chet Singh Bajwa who, in Punjabi parlance, was resting his gun on the Maharajah's shoulder to fire at the people he did not like. For a short while Bajwa succeeded in becoming the power behind the throne. He had the Dogra guard removed from the fort, forbade Dhyan Singh (who had been Chamberlain–*Deodhidar*) and his son Hira Singh access to the Maharajah's apartments. Power turned Bajwa's mind and he became intolerably arrogant. Prince Nao Nihal Singh resented Bajwa's ascendancy as fiercely as did the Dogras, but was engaged in prosecuting the campaign against the Afghans. Gulab Singh Dogra retired to his estate in Jammu and busied himself in consolidating his hold on the hill areas.

The discord between the ministers became an open scandal and disloyal elements began to take advantage of the situation. Mian Rattan Chand and his son Prithi Chand captured several forts in the hills around Nagrota. This uprising was easily quelled by Lehna Singh Majithia, who defeated the Rajputs and brought Rattan Chand and Prithi Chand in chains to Lahore. Prince Nao Nihal Singh's presence at the frontier put new zest into his troops. Till then General Ventura and Captain Wade, who were accompanying the Punjabis, had spent much of their energies quarrelling with each other and had been unable to make any headway against the tribesmen. Prince Nao Nihal Singh took charge of the situation. He appointed

Colonel Sheikh Bassawan to take over command and ordered him to advance. Within a few days, the Punjabis forced their way through the Khyber Pass and captured Ali Masjid. They marched on to Kabul which had fallen on 9th August 1839.

By the end of August 1839, both Prince Nao Nihal Singh and Gulab Singh Dogra were back in Lahore. Wrangling began all over again. The Prince had it conveyed to the Maharajah that it was the considered opinion of all the advisers that Bajwa should be dismissed. The Maharajah not only ignored the advice but made Bajwa's approval a condition precedent for the grant of new *jagirs*. The *Punjab Akhbar* of 25th September 1839 states: 'The Maharajah demanded the reason of Bhais Ram Singh and Gobind Ram's absence. Raja Suchet Singh replied that it was due to the enmity which existed between them and Chet Singh.' Kharak Singh was very angry. He ordered a heavier guard around the palace and warned Chet Singh's regiment to be on the watch at all times with their muskets loaded. He refused to grant his son permission to retire on a *jagir* he wanted. The Prince also spoke in anger. 'I care little about the *jagir*. My care is for the welfare of the state. Let Raja Dhyan Singh remain, but Sardar Chet Singh's interference with any of the affairs of the State is highly improper.'

Prince Nao Nihal Singh decided to take the decisive step. He sounded Mr. Clerk, who was acting as British Agent at Ludhiana in the absence of Col. Wade, and being assured that the British would not create difficulties (Clerk had counselled patience) quietly assumed the functions of the ruler. The Lahore newswriter recorded: 'Nao Nihal Singh holds Durbar twice a day at which hundreds of the first in rank and most respectable attend.'

Kharak Singh tried to retrieve the situation by suggesting that Bajwa and Dhyan Singh Dogra act in concert and persuaded Bajwa to throw himself at the mercy of the Prince. Dhyan Singh refused to collaborate and Nao Nihal remained adamant. Bajwa realised his days were numbered. He could not trust his body-guards and was afraid to leave the side of the Maharajah. Even that did not save him.

In the early hours of the morning of 8th October 1839, there took place the first of a series of murders that were to become a regular feature of the Lahore Durbar. The American, Colonel Gardner (known to the Punjabis as 'Gardauna') who was a Commandant in the Artillery of Raja Dhyan Singh and who accompanied the Dogra on his murderous mission, gives a graphic account of the incident.

According to Gardner, Chet Singh Bajwa had succeeded in winning over General Ventura to his side and had thereupon become openly hostile to the Dogras. The evening preceding the murder he had been rash enough to threaten Dhyan Singh in the Durbar with the words: 'See what will become of you in twenty-four hours.'

Dhyan Singh Dogra had not been inactive. He had been assiduously circulating rumours that Chet Singh had sold the Punjab to the British and had promised to give them six annas of every rupee of the revenue of the State. He had also won over Kharak Singh's wife, Chand Kaur, Prince Nao Nihal Singh, the Sandhawalias and most of the Punjabi officers, including the palace guard to his side before he made his move. On the evening of the 7th of October, the guards at the palace were secretly instructed that 'whatever occurred, whatever thunders there might be at the gates, every one was to feign sleep.' Next morning at three o'clock while the city slept and all was still, save the cries of the chowkidars, '*Khabardar ho*', a party of about fifteen men entered the palace.

'Who is it?' asked a voice.

Dhyan Singh Dogra replied: 'The Maharajah goes tomorrow to bathe at Amristsar, and we are to make the necessary preparations.'

As the party came to the *zenana* apartments where the Maharajah was known to sleep, mysterious hands opened the doors one after another to let the party through. Only at the inner gate did Dhyan Singh have to whisper instructions and even that opened as noiselessly as the others. The party stealthily made its way up a dark flight of stairs, over a place called the *Badsha-i-Takht*, and thence to the royal apartment. The Dogra brothers, Gulab Singh and Dhyan Singh, held a whispered consultation. At that moment a man started up from his sleep, called out and ran for help. Suchet Singh Dogra fired and knocked him down. Gulab Singh spoke angrily, and told off Suchet Singh for his stupidity. There was a commotion and the guards began to run about. Dhyan Singh Dogra rushed out to pacify them. He met the Subedar in command who asked: 'Why did you fire?' Dhyan Singh simply showed his right hand (on which he had two thumbs) and ordered the officer to remain silent. The Subedar pointed to the Royal bed-chamber and the guards quietly returned to their barracks.

The door of the Maharajah's bedroom, the *Khwabgah* or Dreamland, also opened without any command. The whole party entered. The room was dimly lit. The Maharajah was sitting up in his bed; a *gadwai* (waterman) was pouring out water for him to rinse his mouth: he was getting ready to say his morning prayers. The bed alongside on which Chet Singh Bajwa was known to sleep was empty. But the state of the bed-sheets and pillows showed clearly that it had been occupied a very short time before.

'Where is your boon companion?' asked some one in the party. The Maharajah replied truthfully that he had fled on hearing a shot fired. Where, he did not know. He also begged that Chet Singh's life might be spared. He tried to get up to plead with the intruders and prevent them from going further into the *zenana.* He was rudely pushed back to his bed and four men mounted guard to keep him there while others searched the adjoining rooms and passages. Torches were lit and the party broke up into two groups. It seemed that Bajwa had really got away. The party were about to give up the search when one of the men caught the gleam of a shining object at the end of a long, narrow passage. They turned back and caught Chet

Singh in a corner with an unsheathed sword clutched in his shaking hands. He was too terrified to wield the weapon whose glitter had betrayed him. He was dragged out and taken into the presence of his Royal patron. The Maharajah begged his son, Nao Nihal Singh, his kinsmen, the Sandhawalias, and the Dogras to forgive Chet Singh. The Maharahah's hands were pinned behind him where he sat.

'The eyes of Dhyan Singh seemed to shoot fire as his gaze alighted and fixed itself on his deadly foe,' writes Col. Gardner. Gulab Singh stepped in front to dispatch Bajwa with his own hands, but Dhyan Singh roughly shook him off, and dagger in hand, slowly advanced towards his enemy. 'The twenty-four hours you were courteous enough to mention to me have not yet elapsed,' he said grinding his teeth. Then with the spring of a tiger the successful counter-plotter dashed at his enemy and plunged his dagger into Chet Singh's heart, crying out, 'Take this in memory of Ranjit Singh.'

Chapter 2

Death beneath the Gateway

The manner in which Chet Singh Bajwa was murdered left no doubt in Maharajah Kharak Singh's mind that if he did not retire from active life, his end might also be a violent one. In any case the shock of seeing his boon companion disembowelled in his presence was too great for him.

The *Punjab Akhbar* of the morning after the murder records Maharajah Kharak Singh as observing 'that he has nothing to do with the State and its rule, they are all gone with Chet Singh, and that he will be content with his former *jagir,* leaving everything else to Raja Dhyan Singh and Koonwar Nao Nihal Singh.'

The murder of Bajwa was followed by the attachment of his property, the arrest of his brother and the persecution of dignitaries who had been friendly with Chet Singh, notably Misr Beli Ram, the Chief Accountant of the Durbar and custodian of the *Koh-i-noor* diamond, and his brothers, Rup Lal, Kardar of Jullundur, and Megh Raj who was in charge of the State treasury at Gobindgarh. For a time, even General Ventura and Prince Sher Singh were under a cloud because they had refused to join the conspiracy to remove Chet Singh.

Fakir Azizuddin, who had been sent on a secret mission to Simla, was instructed to inform the British of the facts leading to the assassination of Chet Singh and the imprisonment of Beli Ram and his relations.

Maharajah Kharak Singh moved out to his house in the city. Prince Nao Nihal Singh occupied the palace in the fort and became Maharajah of the Punjab in all but name. He was then only eighteen years old.

Nao Nihal Singh was made in a different mould from his father. He did not desire the pomp and paraphernalia of a Maharajah's life and let all the ceremonial functions remain the prerogative of his father towards whom he behaved with courtesy and rectitude. But he made it known to the ministers, governors of provinces and generals, who had got used to being left to themselves by the ailing Ranjit Singh and the lackadaisical Kharak Singh, that he meant to govern the Punjab personally and effectively. They began to chafe under the Prince's iron rule. On the North-West Frontier, the Pathans took advantage of the unsettled state of affairs at Lahore and revolted. Dhyan Singh Dogra moaned that it would have been better for him if he had perished on Ranjit Singh's funeral pyre. Gulab Singh Dogra betook himself on an extended pilgrimage to the sacred cities of Hindustan. Ventura sulked and threatened to resign.

Nao Nihal Singh took these and other matters in his stride. He vigorously suppressed the Pathan tribes. He summoned the Governors of Kashmir and Multan to his presence and reprimanded them for being tardy in paying in the revenues. He ordered Gulab Singh to return home and sent Ventura to the hills. Prince Kashmira Singh was forced to renounce his pretensions to the throne. Bikram Singh Bedi of Una, who enjoyed the prestige of being a descendant of Guru Nanak and had misused his position by taking the law in his own hands, was heavily mulcted. Public works were taken in hand. Trees were planted alongside the road between Lahore and Amritsar and gardens laid out in the suburbs of the two cities. Dhyan Singh came round of his own accord and accepted, however reluctantly, to be one of the Council of Seven Ministers, which included besides him, Fakir Azizuddin, Jemadar Khushal Singh, Bhaia Ram Singh, Ajit Singh Sandhawalia and Lehna Singh Majithia. Within a couple of months the Punjab felt that the spirit of Ranjit Singh had been resurrected in the person of his grandson, Prince Nao Nihal Singh.

The British were unwilling to recognise the *de facto* change in the Government of the Punjab, but their reluctance was overcome by the fact that they wanted permission for their troops in Afghanistan to be allowed to come back through the Punjab. The Durbar was strongly opposed to conceding this request but Nao Nihal Singh overruled his Councillors and thus gained the support of his powerful neighbours. The only conditions made were that the British would not again ask for similar facilities and their troops would avoid passing near the capital. On his way back, the Commander of the British troops, Lord Keane, called on Nao Nihal Siugh at Lahore to thank him for the cooperation the Punjab had given in the Afghan campaign. He was tactfully asked to convey to his Government that Colonel Wade's continued support of Maharajah Kharak Singh was not looked upon with favour by the Council of Ministers. A few weeks later when Colonel Wade himself passed through Lahore on his way back to India, he was not allowed to call on the Maharajah. The British Government's reluctant acquiescence with Nao Nihal Singh's wishes made the Prince sceptical of their professions of good will. Suspicion developed on either side and letters said to have been written by Nao Nihal Singh to Dost Mohammed proposing a joint war against the British, found their way to Calcutta. Nao Nihal Singh disclaimed them as deliberate forgeries. He realised the wisdom of not putting all his eggs in the British basket. The Punjabi newswriter reported from Ferozepur that 'Captain Lawrence was engaged night and day in strengthening the fort and that guns were being provided for it.' The Sardars advised that it would be provident to construct a fort at Kasur. And despite British objections, Nao Nihal allowed the Gurkha General Matabar Singh, who was known to be anti-British, to continue residing in Lahore. The Governor-General realised that he could not bully the Durbar and in April 1840 replaced Col. Wade by Mr. Clerk who was more acceptable to the Durbar. Nao Nihal Singh could now turn his attention to other things. The most important was to reduce the Dogra brothers to their proper size.

Early in May 1840, Zorawar Singh sent a report from Iskardu that in consequence of the disaffection of the people of that country with their ruler, Ahmed Shah, he had helped the son, Mohammed Shah, to replace his father and was firmly established there. Nao Nihal

Singh did not want Zorawar Singh to become a kingmaker in Little Tibet and issued orders for the reinstate- ment of Ahmed Shah, on condition that he sent tribute to Lahore. Zorawar Singh turned to his immediate overlord, Gulab Singh Dogra, and the two devised ways of circumventing the Prince's orders without openly flaunting them.

The Prince realised that the Dogras had become inconveniently powerful. They had the monopoly over the salt mines, which they exploited to great advantage. The Prince expressed a desire to take over the mines so that salt could be sold cheaply all over the Punjab. Before Nao Nihal could take the salt monopoly out of their hands, the Dogras invited their neighbour in the hills, Balbir Sen of Mandi, to revolt against the Durbar. Nao Nihal Singh ordered Ajit Singh Sandhawalia and Ventura—both hostile to the Dogras—to bring the hill Rajputs to obedience. Durbar troops defeated the forces of the hill chiefs, occupied many forts, and brought Balbir Sen as prisoner to Amritsar where he was lodged in Gobindgarh fort. Ventura established a chain of police posts in the hills. Under instructions from Nao Nihal Singh, he abolished the arbitrary taxes levied by the petty Rajas and prohibited the sale of women and children a practice common amongst the poorer sections of the hill people. Ventura's campaign also subdued the Dogras for a while.

During the summer of 1840 the cannons of the fort of Lahore were kept busy firing salvos in honour of victories gamed by Punjabi armies. The people felt that the old days of glory had returned.

The success of the summer was like a lambent flame about to die. The rot as usual began at the top and spread to the entire body politic. Maharajah Kharak Singh, who had been reduced to utter idleness, began to drink harder and consume large quantities of opium till he was reduced to imbecility. Nao Nihal also began to drink more than usual. It was said that the success against Mandi had turned his head. He allowed himself to be surrounded by astrologers, soothsayers and charlatans of that ilk who forecast that he would extend the empire from Kabul to the banks of the Ganges. The Prince let these dreams of grandeur fill his mind.

Opium and alcohol claimed Kharak Singh, who died in the early hours of the morning of 5th November 1840. The guns of the fort began to fire salvos in homage to the departed monarch. Prince Nao Nihal Singh, who was then in his hunting lodge at Shah Bilawal, a couple of miles outside the city, heard the tell-tale boom of cannon. A few minutes later, a dispatch-rider arrrived and confirmed the Prince's fears. Nao Nihal Singh was stung with remorse at the thought that he had not done his duty as a son. He repaired immediately to his father's *haveli.* The consciousness of guilt continued to haunt the Prince. The diarist Sohan Lal records three eerie incidents that happened to Nihal Singh. As he was coming down the steps of his father's *haveli*, he felt a pair of invisible hands grab him by the shoulders. When he turned back to look, there was no one behind him. The second experience was later in the morning when he was walking behind his father's cortege. As the funcral procession passed through Taksali Gate, the Prince felt a heavy blow on his head and collapsed. No one could see the assailant (nor even believed there was one) till the Prince came to and complained that he had felt as if somebody had hit him with a stick. The procession started once again and got safely to the site near Hazuri Bagh near the mausoleum of Ranjit Singh.

Kharak Singh's body was laid on a pile of sandalwood. Two of his widows and eleven maid-servants mounted the pyre. The widows made Nao Nihal Singh and Dhyan Singh Dogra put their hands on the dead Maharajah's chest and swear by all that they held most sacred to serve the State loyally and faithfully. They put the saffron mark on the foreheads of the new Maharajah and the Chief Minister. The last prayer was said and amidst the chanting of Vedic Mantras, Nao Nihal Singh lit the funeral pyre.

After the cremation, the Maharajah went to the Ravi: a branch of the river ran close by the ramparts of the fort. While he was taking the ceremonial post-funeral bath, a mulberry tree which stood near the bank suddenly came down with a thunder-clap. It was an old and withered tree which had been unable to stand the strain of having dozens of people climbing on it to see the funeral. But Nao Nihal Singh was very perturbed because he heard the wail of human voices come out of the tree as it fell.

The Maharajah's nerves were highly wrought. On his way back he took the hand of Udham Singh, the son of Gulab Singh Dogra. Other courtiers followed behind them. Then the fourth and final incident took place. This one, however, was no fanciful chimera of the Prince's tortured mind.

The party passed by Kharak Singh's funeral pyre, now blazing fiercely, and came to the *Roshnai Durwaza*—the Gate of Splendour. Just as Nao Nihal Singh was passing underneath, the arch of the gate gave way and slabs of stone and masonry crashed down on his head. Sohan Lal Suri, the official chronicler of the Lahore Durbar, narrates the incident in some detail: 'After this the Kanwar came near the gate. Suddenly, somebody from the unknown flung the whole of the roof along with bricks and limestone, like an arrow of death, on the top of the Kanwar's head, and as divinely ordained, the brain was at once crushed to pieces. Thick blood gushed out and the blessed body was buried under the debris of bricks and limestone. Mian Udham Singh gave up his life to its Giver and the other companions, viz. the Raja Kalan (Dhyan Singh Dogra), the Bhais, Dewan Dina Nath and other such dignitaries, received injuries on their heads, shoulders and backs from the masonry. Government officials extricated the Blessed Body from the heap and were much pained and grieved to see the Kanwar's condition. The mirror of sense was shattered to pieces by the stone of mishap.'

Nao Nihal Singh was brought to Ranjit Singh's mausoleum where Bhai Gobind Ram and his brother

Ram Singh, who had only received superficial injuries, examined the Maharajah's pulse. It was obvious that life was fast ebbing out. Raja Dhyan Singh Dogra, being the Chief Minister, took command of the situation. He ordered the Prince to be carried to the palace in a palanquin and had the gates of the fort shut against every one else—even members of the Royal family. But first he sent for the Royal physician, the Hungarian Dr. Martin Honigberger.

Dr. Honigberger arrived within a few mintues. He later made a record of this visit to the Hazuri Bagh: 'The Prince was on his bed, his head most awfully crushed and his state was such that no hope of recovery existed. With that conviction I left the tent, and whispered to the minister, in so low a tone that no one else could hear it, "Medical art can do nothing to relieve the unfortunate prince"; upon which the minister requested me to wait there while he re-entered the tent, and, after a short stay therein, he came out, addressing me loud enough to be heard by all the assembly, who listened attentively, asking "whether they might give some soup to the Koonwar Saheb," (Royal-Prince), he wishing to have some. Whereupon I answered, "Of course; he is in need only of parsley"; a proverb applied to those dangerously ill, and not expected to live. The minister's intention in questioning me thus, was to conceal at that moment the approaching death of the prince in order to have time to make the necessary preparations, so that the peace and tranquillity of the country might not be disturbed, in which he succeeded so that the death of the Prince remained a secret for three days. This interval he took advantage of to recall Sher Singh, and place him upon the throne.'

At that time no one had any doubt that the fall of the arch had been an accident. The steps taken by Dhyan Singh to keep Nao Nihal Singh's death a secret were however misconstrued by mischief-makers. Honigberger heard of the stories that had got round and wrote; 'It would have been proper at the time to have made enquiries whether the falling of the wall by which Nao Nihal Singh and Oottum Singh had been crushed, was accidental, or a premeditated machination of wicked conspirators; but none thought it worth their while to make the enquiry . . .'

The official British report of the incident, based on the information immediately forwarded by their newswriter in Lahore, mentions it to have been an accident.

Col. Gardner is however certain that the whole thing was contrived by Raja Dhyan Singh Dogra. Since he claimed to be present at the time, what he says deserves to be carefully read—particularly as his version is accepted by many serious historians, both English and Punjabi. Gardner writes: 'The *palki*-bearers who had carried Nao Nihal Singh to his palace were sent to their homes; they were servants in my own company of Artillery, and were five in number. Two were afterwards privately put to death, two escaped into Hindustan, the fate of the fifth is unknown to me. One of the *palki*-bearers afterwards affirmed that when the Prince was put into the *palki,* and when he was assisting to put him there, he saw that above the right ear there was a wound which bled so slightly as only to cause a blotch of blood about the size of a rupee on the pillow or cloth on which Nao Nihal Singh's head rested while in the *palki*. Now it is a curious fact that when the room was opened, in which his corpse was first exposed by Dhian Singh, blood in great quantities, both in fluid and coagulated pools, was found around the head of the cloth on which the body lay. Be this as it may, when the doors were thrown open the Sindhanwalias found the young Maharajah dead, Dhyan Singh prostrate in affliction on the ground, and Fakir Nuruddin, the Royal physician, lamenting that all remedies had been useless.'

There is not the slightest doubt that Col. Gardner has used his imagination to convert a tragic accident into a dastardly conspiracy–because the facts prove it clearly to have been an accident and nothing else. It is not unlikely that the old Roshnai Gate had been severely shaken by the blast of cannon firing continuously for over five hours close by and by the pressure of the crowds which had taken every point of vantage to watch the funeral. There is nothing to suggest that the arch giving way was not an act of Providence. For one, Kharak Singh died at about 9 a.m. and was cremated a few hours later at a spot which was a public thoroughfare, being the site of the cremation of Ranjit Singh and alongside the most frequented Sikh temple in the city. With all the coming and going of people and the preparation of the funeral pyre of Kharak Singh, it is inconceivable that any one could have had the time or the opportunity to fit in something in the archway which would make it collapse at a given signal. And it is hardly likely that Dhyan Singh would have sacrificed the life of his nephew, allowed himself and others to be injured, risk the vengeance of the populace of Lahore and yet be unprepared for the eventuality.

Nao Nihal Singh's death was clearly an act of God. But why did the Guru deprive the kingdom of the one man who might have restored to it the glory it had in the days of Maharajah Ranjit Singh?

Chapter 3

The Ambitious Widow

The deaths of Maharajah Kharak Singh and Nao Nihal Singh within a few hours of each other caused a crisis of unparalleled magnitude in the Lahore Durbar. The Chief Minister, Dhyan Singh Dogra, handled it with all the ability at his command. When Nao Nihal Singh had succumbed to his injuries, the Dogra ordered that the news should not be announced till the matter of succession was settled. He arranged for food to be brought from the royal kitchen to the room where the Maharajah lay cold and dead on the floor and for empty plates to be taken out. Visitors were turned back on the plea that the doctors had advised complete rest. Even Nao Nihal's mother, widowed only a few hours earlier, was refused admission and gave vent to her rage by hammering at the iron gates of the fort with her bare hands.

Dhyan Singh sent for Fakir Azizuddin and Jemadar Khushal Singh and, having ascertained their wishes and the approval of Bhaia Ram Singh, sent word to Prince Sher Singh at Batala to come to Lahore immediately and take over as the Maharajah of the Punjab.

Sher Singh was the fittest person to succeed to the throne. He was popular with the army, he was courteous and amiable, and the English, whose opinions were of consequence in the Durbar's affairs, were known to approve of him.

The confidence that Dhyan Singh Dogra had placed in his fellow courtiers was betrayed by Bhaia Ram Singh, who not only let out the secret of Nao Nihal Singh's death but along with his brother Bhaia Gobind Ram decided to put up Kharak Singh's window, Chand Kaur, as a rival candidate. They sent word to her and Sandhawalia kinsmen, Attar Singh, who was living in retirement at Hardwar, and Ajit Singh, who was with the army in Kulu, to come to Lahore at once.

Dhyan Singh Dogra tried frantically to get some sort of agreement from Chand Kaur before the intriguers' brew came to boiling point. He temporarily succeeded in persuading Chand Kaur to accept the honorific title of *Raj-Mata*–Queen Mother–and allow Sher Singh to become Maharajah. Even before Sher Singh arrived in Lahore, Dhyan Singh summoned the British agent, Maulvi Rajab Ali, and in the presence of all the courtiers (including the Bhais) asked him to convey to his Government that the arrangement had been 'adopted by the whole Khalsa in concord and unanimity'. The Maulvi reported that the assemblage had applauded the statement with the words, 'the Khalsa on this subject were unanimous heart and soul.'

A few hours after the meeting, Prince Sher Singh arrived in Lahore. The death of Nao Nihal Singh was made known and the succession of the new Maharajah was proclaimed.

In the afternoon Nao Nihal Singh's body was taken to the spot where his father's ashes still smouldered. Two of his consorts mounted the pyre with him. One pinned the royal aigrette on Sher Singh's turban; the other daubed Dhyan Singh Dogra's forehead with saffron to signify his being Chief Minister. The *Satis* made the Prince and the minister swear loyalty to the State before they perished in the flames.

On 11th November another melancholy procession wound its way through the streets of Lahore. It was led by the late Maharajah's favourite elephant. The howdah bore two caskets containing the ashes of Maharajah Kharak Singh and Nao Nihal Singh. Rich people threw expensive shawls over the urns; the poor paid their homage with flowers. The cavalcade went out of Delhi Gate on the Grand Trunk Road towards Amritsar and on to Hardwar. Thus the remains of the father and son, who had found it difficult to live together, mingled in the holy river.

Two actors were gone, but two others took their place on the Durbar stage; Chand Kaur and Sher Singh.

The sanctimonious Bhais, Ram Singh and Gobind Ram, found a willing tool in Chand Kaur. Under their advice she refused to accept Sher Singh's succession and sent for Gulab Singh Dogra from Jammu to counteract the influence of his brother Dhyan Singh. Dhyan Singh suggested many compromises. She could marry Sher Singh, or, now being childless, adopt Sher Singh's son Pertap Singh. The widow spurned the offer of marriage. How could she marry a man whom she had contemptuously described as the bastard son of a water-carrier (*choba*), or a dyer (*cheemba*)? She parried the suggestion of adopting Pertap by offering instead to adopt Dhyan Singh Dogra's son, Hira Singh. She also had it noised about that one of Nao Nihal Singh's widows was pregnant. Dhyan Singh did not fall into the trap of having his son adopted by the Queen mother and made a last appeal to Chand Kaur to preserve the State. He placed his turban at her feet and implored her to accept an arrangement that he and Fakir Azizudin had thought out as a compromise; she would be the Queen Regent and Sher Singh the head of a Council of Regency. Chand Kaur indignantly tore up the proposal. Dhyan Singh threw in the sponge. In a stormy scene in the crowded Durbar he warned Chand Kaur of the danger of lending an ear to mischief-makers and told her that the Government of the Punjab did not depend either on her or on Sher Singh or any of the claimants in the Royal family because it was the government of the entire Khalsa.

A few days later, the two Sandhawalia Sardars, Ajit Singh and Attar Singh, arrived in Lahore and took over control. Behind them was Gulab Singh Dogra and the Bhais. An agreement was drafted on 27th November by which Sher Singh was to return to his estate in Mukerian for eight months, leaving his son Pertap Singh as hostage in Lahore. If Nao Nihal Singh's widow bore a son, he would be acknowledged as the heir; if she did not, a new agreement would be drawn up. Sixteen leading noblemen–Sikh, Hindu and Muslim–signed the *Ikrarnamah*.

Chand Kaur was formally installed with the title of *Malika Mukaddas* (Queen Empress), and all the courtiers including Sher Singh, who had been nominally made President of the Council of Ministers, and Dhyan Singh Dogra, who continued to be described as Chief Minister, paid her tribute. This was on 2nd December 1840.

The next day Sher Singh left Lahore to return to his estate. He was promised an allowance of Rs. 1 lakh per year and an additional *jagir* of the same sum. These did not, however, distract his mind from the throne and he set about winning over support for his cause.

Chand Kaur took Sher Singh's place as Resident of the Council of four ministers: Attar Singh Sandhawalia, Jemadar Khushal Singh, Lehna Singh Majithia and Raja Dhyan Singh.

A few days after Sher Singh's departure, the Prince's chief supporter, Raja Dhyan Singh Dogra, was involved in an incident which proved to him that the Mai–the title by which Chand Kaur came to be known amongst the people–did not need his services. He was going towards the private apartments, which was his right as Chamberlain, when the guard stationed by Ajit Singh Sandhawalia barred his way. This led to an exchange of abuse between the Dogra and the Sandhawalia. The Mai supported Ajit Singh and thus made it clear to Dhyan Singh that he was no longer to consider himself *Deodhidar*. Rather than become embroiled in more intrigue, Dhyan Singh also left Lahore early in January 1841 for his home in the estate of Jammu. He wrote to Prince Sher Singh assuring him of his support and advising him to make contacts with officers of the regiments posted at Lahore.

The Mai and the Sandhawalias had the run of affairs for a few days. But the dice were heavily loaded against them. They did their best to win over the army and get the cooperation of ministers. But neither one nor the other could quite reconcile themselves to being ruled by a woman who could not leave the veiled seclusion of the *zenana.*

Chand Kaur's first move was to get her powerful neighbours, the English, to recognise her succession. She proposed sending a mission to the Governor-General with presents for Queen Victoria. The idea of the mission was dropped as the British, who still needed Punjabi collaboration to pursue their aggression against Kabul, readily accorded her government *de facto* recognition.

While recognising the Mai's government, the English were contemplating taking over her kingdom. The British attitude towards an ally who had not only helped them to win the war in Afghanistan but was allowing his territory to be used by alien armies as if it were a common highway, is an example of ingratitude the like of which would be hard to find in the pages of history books. Sir William Macnaghten proposed that the British should unilaterally declare the Treaty of 1809 null and void, take Peshawar from the Punjabis and give it to the Durranis. He also suggested that the Punjab should be further divided into two: the hills should be administered by the Dogras and the plains by the Sandhawalias. The Governor-General counselled patience and comforted Macnaghten with the thought that in the near future the Punjab would disintegrate and then all the Durbar territory across the Indus could be attached and given to their Durrani puppet.

The chief problem of the Mai was the loyalty of the Army. Sher Singh was popular with the troops and with the European officers. Soldiers were reported to be leaving the cantonments to join the Prince at Batala. Chand Kaur tried to hold back the ebbing tide by tempting the troops with gold. She appointed Tej Singh Commander-in-Chief and through him assured the men that their wages would be paid regularly on the 25th of every month. She made the men and officers swear allegiance to her. But none of these measures helped her. Sher Singh offered an increase in wages and desertions began on a larger scale than ever. Within a fortnight of her assumption of power she had to have two battalions posted inside the fort for her safety.

The Governors of the distant provinces failed to send the revenue in time and the soldiers were not even paid their first month's wages as promised. The desertions became general; the few soldiers that remained in Lahore refused to obey officers loyal to the Mai. Unpaid soldiery ran riot in the countryside helping themselves at the expense of the poor peasantry.

Then the rumour spread that the British Army was marching towards the frontier. There was panic in the Punjab.

Sher Singh decided to take over power from the feeble hands of the widow and save the Punjab from disintegration. He sent a secret envoy to Mr. Clerk at Ludhiana to get British reactions to his bid for the throne. The British were bogged down in Afghanistan and badly needed assistance. In the Anglophile Sher Singh they saw a potential ally and gave him assurance of support.

Sher Singh left Batala on 14th January 1841 at the head of an army composed of deserters who had flocked to his standard. He pitched his camp at *Budhu da Ava* just outside Lahore. Col. Gardner describes his arrival at the city outskirts: 'The most tremendous roars that ever rose from a concourse of human beings drowned our voices, distant as it was, and warned us that the man had arrived. Sher Singh had indeed come, and planted his flag and pitched his camp on the high mound called *Budhu da ava*. The whole of his troops then thundered a salute, which continued for two hours, amid shouts of 'Sher Singh Badshah! Dhyan Singh Wazir! Death to Chand Kaur and the Dogras!'

The Mai decided to fight it out. She dismissed Tej Singh, who was disliked by the soldiers, and appointed Gulab Singh Dogra as administrator and defender of the city. She cleared four months' arrears in the soldiers' wages and lavished presents of gold bangles, necklaces, jewels and shawls on the officers. She issued orders to the city s bankers forbidding them to lend money to Sher Singh. These measures had the reverse effect. The troops sensed the Mai's nervousness and felt that she was trying to gain a lost cause by bribery. Sher Singh did not have much money but he was able to infuse confidence that his was the winning side and he would be able to redeem his promise of a permanent increase of Re. 1 per month in the wages of the troops as well as reward those who joined them. The Mai's regiments stationed outside the city walls went over in a body to Sher Singh. The regiment guarding the magazine refused to supply her gunners with powder. Sher Singh had 26,000 infantry, 8,000 horses and 45 guns. The Mai was left with only 5,000 men and a limited quantity of gunpowder.

On 15th January 1841, Sher Singh moved up from Shalamar Gardens towards Lahore. The gates of the city were forced open at night and many bazars were looted by his troops. Early on the morning of the 16th, Sher Singh entered Lahore. Amongst the officers with him were the Europeans Ventura, Court and Van Cortlandt. He made a belated proclamation assuring safety of life and property to the citizens and offered pardon to those who would leave the Mai's service and come over to him. By the evening, the leading Sardars, including Sham Singh Attariwala, Fakir Azizuddin and the two Bhais, Gobind Ram and Ram Singh, who had instigated the Mai to stake her claim, made their submission. They forwarded a joint appeal to the Mai and Gulab Singh Dogra to lay down their arms.

The Mai supported by Gulab Singh Dogra and the Sandhawalias refused to make an unconditional surrender. On 16th January, Sher Singh's guns opened concentrated fire on the southern bastion of the fort. The defenders hit back, firing indiscriminately over the city. The bombardment continued for two days and many breaches were made in the three-hundred-year-old ramparts of the fort. The Dogras fought back stoutly and repelled attempts to rush the citadel. For two days the citizens of Lahore lived in peril of their lives. The bazars were cluttered with the debris of fallen houses; the stink of decaying corpses and carcases of animals became unbearable. Both sides had had enough of the fight—particularly the defenders of the fort, who had now to contend with snipers mounted on the minarets of the Badshahi Mosque which overlooked the palace courtyard. In the forty-eight hours of fighting nearly five thousand people were killed and almost half the houses of the city damaged.

On the evening of 17th January 1841, Dhyan Singh Dogra arrived in Lahore and arranged a cease-fire the next day. He and Fakir Azizuddin began negotiations for a settlement. The Mai was promised a *jagir* of Rs. 7 lakhs a year and allowed to retain a part of her husband's treasure in exchange for the surrender of the fort. Sher Singh undertook to show her the respect due to a brother's widow and agreed to retain the services of the men who had sided with her. The Mai's resistance was broken and with tears in her eyes she put her signature to the document. Her short reign of a month and a half was over.

At midnight Gulab Singh and his Dogras evacuated the fort, taking with them all the Durbar's treasure kept at

Lahore. It is said that sixteen carts were loaded with gold, silver and bullion and five hundred bags of gold mohurs were removed from the fort treasury.

Gulab Singh paid his homage to Sher Singh and handed over the *Koh-i-noor* diamond to him. The Dogra was given leave to go to the North-West Frontier to help the British armies engaged in the Afghan campaign. The Sandhawalias were too proud to bend their knees before Sher Singh. Attar Singh and his nephew Ajit Singh sought asylum in British territory. Ajit Singh tried to see Clerk at Ludhiana and having failed with him, proceeded to Calcutta to see the Governor-General himself. Lehna Singh Sandhawalia was arrested and put in the dungeon.

The next day Sher Singh entered the fort to the salute of the guns. His first act was to pay his respects to the deposed Mai, Chand Kaur.

The widow paid dearly for her ambition. After her deposition, she not only acknowledged Sher Singh as Maharajah of the Punjab, but in order to retain her position agreed to marry him. It was decided that the nuptials should take place after a decent lapse of time. Chand Kaur moved out to a house in the city to await the day when Sher Singh would take her back to the palace as his Maharani.

That day was not destined to dawn. One sultry day in the month of June, while the Maharajah was away in

Batala, Chand Kaur got an attack of migraine and asked her maid-servants for medicine. Chand Kaur had reason to suspect that the medicine was tinctured with poison and threw it away. At night while she was resting, the same women stole into her apartments and smashed her skull with a grindstone. They were apprehended next morning, but instead of being made to confess, had their tongues pulled out and then executed.

Who ordered the murder of the unfortunate widow? Local gossip named Maharajah Sher Singh, Dhyan Singh Dogra, as well as his elder brother, Gulab Singh. Diarist Sohan Lal accuses Sher Singh and Dhyan Singh and states that Mohan Singh, Thanedar of Lahore, had hired four women (Hiro the bald, Aso, Bhari the cobbler's wife, and Hasso of Fatehgarh) to commit the foul deed and that the murder had been kept a secret for three days. According to Sohan Lal, the hirelings had only their hands, noses and ears chopped off and while they were being led out of the city, they sobbed out their story to the crowds.

Sohan Lal's version is not supported by newswriters of the different states in the Durbar; nor does the relationship the Mai had with Sher Singh and Dhyan Singh warrant that conclusion. Sohan Lal is unduly harsh on Sher Singh—whom he also accuses of arranging the abortion of Nao Nihal Singh's widow. If one can draw an inference from motives, the only person who could have been worried by the Mai's impending marriage to Sher Singh was Gulab Singh Dogra. He had robbed the palace of its treasure on the pretext of keeping it in safe custody for Chand Kaur. He had also been appointed by her to manage her estates at Kudi Kudiali which adjoined his territories. With one grindstone, Gulab Singh Dogra not only silenced the voice which could have told the sordid truth but also became master of all that he had taken from the fort and of Kudi Kudiali.

Chapter 4

The Dilettante Prince

Prince Sher Singh had always been popular with the army and the common people. He was handsome and courteous. He was a bit of a dilettante and dressed with meticulous care. He used expensive perfumes and applied pomades to curl his moustache and set his beard—which he parted in the middle and tucked upwards towards his ears. He liked good food and French wines. He was fond of women and women were fond of him. He admired the English and the English preferred him to any of the other claimants—except the Sandhawalias, who were eager to have the British extend their conquest over the Punjab. But the Sandhawalias were not princes of royal blood and if there was one thing the Punjabis were not willing to forgive, it was a suggestion that their State become a British protectorate.

On 27th January 1841, ten days after his triumphal entry into Lahore, Sher Singh was crowned Maharajah of the Punjab. His son Pertap Singh was proclaimed heir-apparent and Dhyan Singh Dogra became, once again, the Chief Minister.

Despite his universal popularity, Sher Singh's rule began badly. The army had helped him to power on his undertaking to clear the arrears and to increase the pay of the soldiers. When Sher Singh occupied the fort, he discovered the treasury was completely empty; Gulab Singh Dogra had cleaned out everything there was. The soldiers refused to be put off by further promises and proceeded to help themselves or turn against the officers whom they suspected of having made money.

Four days after their entry into the fort, Sher Singh and Dhyan Singh invited the soldiers to the *Summum Burj* (octagonal tower where the durbar was often held)–two men each from every company, troop and gun–to consult with them. The men agreed to do so on condition that no officers should be present. This was conceded and at the first meeting the Maharajah and the minister received only the elected *Panches.* The *Panches* complained of the dishonesty of regimental *munshies* (accountants) and officers in disbursing wages. The Maharajah agreed to replace those specifically named. But he refused to transfer officers the *Panches* did not like. The meeting became stormy. The weak-willed Sher Singh threw up his hands with the remark, '*Kacha Pakka Sambhalo*' (literally, 'raw or ripe it's all yours), which gave the *Panches* to understand that they were free to settle things for themselves. They began to plunder the shopkeepers. 'For six to eight weeks', writes Sohan Lal, the city of Lahore was turned into a veritable hell.' The troops went berserk and began to murder regimental accountants and officers–the chief target being the Europeans, most, if not all, of whom were in communication with the British Agent in Ludhiana. Two Europeans, Col. Foulkes and Major Ford were shot dead by their troops. Ventura's house had to be guarded by three regiments loyal to Sher Singh. Court, who had hidden himself in Ventura's house, barely escaped with his life and fled across the Sutlej. Avitabile had to leave Peshawar and seek the protection of the Afghans at Jalalabad. The wrath of the soliders did not spare the Punjabi officers. In Kashmir, the Governor, Col. Meehan Singh, and in Amritsar, the Garrison Commander, Sobha Singh, were murdered. At Lahore, Jemadar Khushal Singh, his nephew Tej Singh and Lehna Singh Majithia, all of whom were suspected of having British sympathies, had to barricade themselves in their houses.

Sher Singh's difficulties gave Mr. Clerk, the British Agent at Ludhiana, the opportunity to meddle in the affairs of the Durbar. He sent word to Sher Singh that the British Government would like him to be gentle with Mai Chand Kaur (a suggestion he forestalled by having proposed marriage to her) and to make peace with the Sandhawalias. Clerk gave his suggestion an element of blackmail by allowing Ajit Singh Sandhawalia to take up residence close to the Punjab frontier.

Unrest in the Punjab continued unabated. It came to such a pass that the British Agent planned to march to Lahore with an army of 12,000 men. He proposed annexing the Durbar's cis-Sutlej possessions and taking a sum of Rs. 40 lakhs as the price of restoring order. When the news of this proposal leaked out (or was deliberately let out) there was an outburst of anti-British feeling in the Punjab and men like Lehna Singh Majithia, who was known to be friendly to the British, had to quit the State. Maharajah Sher Singh vehemently denied that he had any knowledge of Clerk's proposals. But he was unable to quell the disturbances. With the army in open mutiny, the best Sher Singh could do was to plead with the men to be reasonable. He undertook to redeem his promise of an increase of Re 1 a month in pay and another month's pay as reward. The troops insisted on the clearance of nine months' arrears of wages plus rewards and made a not too veiled threat that if their demands were not conceded, they would depose Sher Singh as they had deposed the Mai. Instead of facing the mutineers resolutely Sher Singh sought escape in the cup and in the company of courtesans. What the Punjab had prayed for was a dictator; what it got was a handsome and well-meaning dandy who knew more about vintage wines and the ways of women than he did of statecraft.

Ajit Singh Sandhawalia was informed of Sher Singh's discomfiture and made attempts to get the British to intervene. Sher Singh counteracted this move by opening negotiations with the British. The sordid drama of intrigue and dealing with foreign elements destroyed the confidence that the people had reposed in the Royal family. A few days after Clerk had made his proposals to enter the Punjab with an army, the people had another opportunity to see how far the Maharajah and the nobility were willing to go to appease foreigners. The British had requested transit facilities for the harems of Shah Shuja and Shah Zaman across the Punjab to Afghanistan. The permit was readily granted and the royal seraglios of several hundred women, eunuchs and bodyguard under the command of Major Broadfoot proceeded on their northern journey. The Durbar supplied an escort of Mussulman troops to go with the cavalcade. The attitude of Major Broadfoot was aggressive from the very start and on more than one occasion he ordered his escort to open fire on Punjabi troops who happened to come near his party. There was no retaliation by the Durbar–not even when Broadfoot crossed the Indus and called on the Pathan tribesmen to revolt against Punjabi domination. Even General Ventura, who had the confidence of the British was ashamed of Broadfoot's behaviour. Capt. J. D. Cunningham, the celebrated author of the *History of the Sikhs*, who had personal cognisance of the facts, wrote: 'It did not appear that his (Broadfoot's) apprehension had even a plausible foundation . . . The whole proceeding merely served to irritate and excite the distrust of the Sikhs generally, and to give Sher Singh an opportunity of pointing out to his mutineer soldiers that the Punjab was surrounded by English armies both ready and willing to make war upon them.'

Had the English decided to make war upon the Punjab? It would appear that even if there was no concrete plan to lauch an invasion (probably because the Durbar was collaborating with them in the Afghan campaign) annexation of the Punjab in the near future was being openly talked of in British circles. In a personal letter on 26th May 1841, Mrs. Henry Lawrence, wife of the chief British expert on the Punjab and the man destined to be the first Resident, wrote: 'Wars, rumours of war, are on every side and there seems no doubt that the next cold weather will decide the long suspended question of occupying the Punjab. Henry, both in his civil and military capacity, will probably be called on to take part in whatever goes on.'

The Broadfoot episode, coming at the end of several months of rumours of betrayal of national interests by the courtiers, noblemen and officers, finally decided the men of the Punjab army that they should make their own voice heard in matters of State. The only institution they were familiar with was the *Panchayat*—the Council of elders which regulated the affairs of the villages from which they came. This institution took an increasingly central place in the affairs of the army and the *Panches* would first deliberate on the orders of the commanding officer and then come back to the men with their recommendations. The results were disastrous. The army lost its discipline as well as direction by officers who had greater experience of military affairs than the elected *Panches*. And soon after, the chief function of the *Panches* became the demanding of higher wages and rewards for their men.

The one point on which the Durbar, the officers and the men were agreed was that nothing was worse than keeping the army inactive. General Zorawar Singh had already glimpsed the plateaus beyond the Himalayas. He was encouraged to go ahead by his immediate overlord, Gulab Singh Dogra who, after the murder of Colonel Meehan Singh, the Governor of Kashmir, had acquired possession of the Valley of the Jhelum. Equipped with the Durbar's troops and forces of the hill chieftains, Zorawar Singh began the second phase of the Punjab's conquest of Tibetan provinces.

There were economic reasons for choosing to extend the frontiers of the Punjab beyond the Himalayas. In the past, Tibetan caravans had passed through the vale of Kashmir on their way to India. Since the British had extended their frontier to the Sutlej, a new route had been opened through the State of Bushair. The worst sufferers were Kashmiri shawl-makers, who got much of their raw wool from Ladakh and Lhasa. The Kashmiri wool industry was facing a crisis and unless Tibetan shepherds were persuaded or compelled to bring their wares to Kashmir markets, there was danger of the industry dying out. By pushing the frontier further up to the source of the Indus and the Sutlej, the Punjab could also exploit the mineral resources in the province of Garo. The Rothak district of Garo was reputed to be rich in gold, borax, sulphur and rock-salt and had a thriving market supplying many parts of Central Asia. There were complementary political reasons alongside the compelling economic ones. By striking out north and then eastwards, the Punjab would ensure itself against the possibility of British encirclement by having a common frontier with the only other independent state of India, Nepal. The venture had the enthusiastic support of Gulab Singh Dogra because he knew that an extension of the Punjab in that direction would inevitably mean the extension of his domains.

A wedge had already been driven into Tibet in 1834 when Zorawar Singh had taken Ladakh. Ranjit Singh had forbidden him to go any further for fear of incurring the wrath of the Chinese Emperor. Since the occupation of Ladakh had not aroused the Chinese overlords, Prince Nao Nihal Singh had allowed Zorawar Singh to drive the wedge a little farther. Iskardu, at the junction of two tributaries of the Indus, was taken from Ahmed Shah. Another approach route to these mountainous regions had been opened up by the occupation of Mandi and Kulu. Sher Singh decided to press these points further: one northwards and the other eastwards towards the Nepalese frontier.

It was not hard to find an excuse for aggression. In April 1841, Zorawar Singh demanded Garo's adhesion to the Punjab as Garo was a dependency of Iskardu and Iskardu was now a province of the Punjab. He also desired that in view of the changed circumstances Lhasa should pay tribute to Lahore rather than to Peking. The Governor of Garo tried to appease Zorawar Singh with gifts of horses and mules. Zorawar Singh declined the gifts and proceeded to Garo itself. One column marched eastwards along the Kumaon Hills and cut off British contact with Lhasa. In June 1841, the Punjabis captured the town of Garo. Zorawar Singh thought it politic to send information of the fact to the Raja of Bushair, who was under British protection. From Garo, Zorawar Singh marched forward towards Tuklakote. A Tibetan force sent to oppose the Punjabi advance was virtually annihilated at

Dogpoo Barmah on 29th August 1841, and ten days later, the Durbar's flag was hoisted at Tuklakote. The Punjabis had, like the Indus itself, pierced the heart of Tibet to its very core. By the time they were able to consolidate their new conquests, the campaigning season was over; the chill winds presaged the coming of winter snow.

This brilliant feat of arms alarmed the British more than the Chinese and they registered a protest with the Lahore Durbar. Sher Singh replied politely that Punjabi intentions had been misunderstood. 'No,' insisted Clerk emphatically in a note of 28th September 1841: 'You yourself are the responsible party in any misunderstanding arising with the British Government out of proceedings of this nature towards Tibet or China or Nepal.' Three weeks later the British Agent demanded that the Punjabis give up their conquests in the province of Lhasa and withdraw to Ladakh by 10th December 1841.

While the verbal warfare was going on between Ludhiana and Lahore, the Chinese were mustering their armies for the defence of Lhasa. With the first fall of snow they encircled the Punjabi advance post, cut off its supply lines, and waited patiently to let the elements do the rest.

Zorawar Singh and his men were reduced to desperate straits. They were marooned at a height of 12,000 feet in the midst of a vast sea of drifting snow and ice. They ran out of food and fuel and soldiers began to die of frost-bite. Zorawar Singh offered to withdraw, but the Chinese were unwilling to let a trapped bird slip out of their grasp. 'You seized Ladakh and we remained silent. You became bold in consequence and took possession of Gartoke and Tuklakote. If you desire peace, give up Ladakh and go back to your own country', was the Chinese reply.

The Punjabis were compelled to try to fight their way out. Hunger and cold had sapped their vitality and they had to contend with an enemy who not only outnumbered them by ten to one but was also equipped for winter warfare. On 12th December 1841, fell the gallant Zorawar Singh. His second-in-command, Rai Singh, agreed to lay down arms on a solemn undertaking by the Chinese that the Punjabis would be allowed to retire unmolested. But as soon as their muskets were handed in, they were butchered in cold blood. The Punjabis at Tuklakote heard of the fate that had befallen their comrades and their brave general and decided to withdraw to their base. Before the spring thaw, the Chinese had reoccupied their Tibetan possessions and reinstated their satellites at Iskardu and Ladakh. Only at Leh the Punjab flag still fluttered defiantly in the Tibetan breeze.

The news of the disaster in Tibet roused the Punjabis and Dogras to action. Since Gulab Singh was the chief most concerned, he rushed reinforcements towards Ladakh and also approached the British for help (most probably to allay their fears). The Governor-General, Lord Ellenborough, disapproved of the project as it might 'have the result of bringing armies from beyond those mountains into India'.

By the spring (1842), reinforcements had reached Leh. The Chinese forces retreated before the Punjabis and in May Ladakh was recaptured. The advance continued in the form of a pincer movement towards Garo. One Punjabi column reached the boundary of the district in August 1842 but was dissuaded from proceeding further by a British officer, Lt. Cunningham, who happened to be there. The other column encircled a Chinese force sent against it from Lhasa, flooded the enemy out of their entrenched positions and then decimated them. The Chinese Commander was taken prisoner.

The Punjabis had more than made up for the defeat of the previous winter. They had also learnt that they could not hold these regions in the winter months and that the British objection to their extension of Punjab power in Tibet was more than academic. On 17th October 1842, the envoys of the Durbar and Gulab Singh's personal representative signed a treaty with the representatives of the Chinese Emperor at Lhasa. It was agreed that the boundaries of Ladakh and Lhasa would be considered inviolable by either party and that the trade, particularly of tea and *pashmina* wool, would, as in the past, pass through Ladakh.

The British had every intention of following up their protests against the Punjab by action, but before they could plan their strategy, events in Afghanistan compelled them not only to overlook Punjabi aggressiveness but to beg for their assistance. In the autumn of 1841 while the Chinese were planning to evict the Punjabis from Tibet, the Afghans rose and destroyed the British army of occupation in their country. Amongst those who were murdered in cold blood was Sir Alexander Burnes, the chief architect of British expansionism in Sindh, the Punjab and Afghanistan. The attempt to put Shah Shuja on the throne of Kabul had been a joint Punjabi–British venture and consequently the disaster which overwhelmed British arms at Kabul could not be overlooked by the Punjab Government. Despite its difficulties in Tibet, the Durbar ordered General Avitabile, who was posted in Peshawar, to go to the relief of the British. The British were surprised at the Punjab's willing cooperation, as their advisers, Wade, Clerk and Shahamat Ali, had told them that no faith should be put in the Punjabis' professions of friendship.

Punjabi troops recaptured Ali Masjid beyond the Khyber but were unable to hold it as winter came on. But as soon as the passes were cleared of snow in the spring of 1842, they again took the offensive and helped the British contingent coming from a different direction to recapture Ali Masjid. The Governor-General, Lord Ellenborough, in an official notification of 19th April expressed his entire satisfaction with the conduct of the troops of Maharajah Sher Singh. He informed his army 'that the loss sustained by the Sikhs in the assault of the Pass which was forced by them is understood to have been equal to that sustained by the troops of Her Majesty to the Government of India'. Ellenborough instructed his Agent at Lahore to offer his congratulations on this occasion, so honourable to the Sikh Army.

The Durbar arranged for the supply of grain, cattle and other provisions to British troops and forwarded its own contingent, which was larger than the British, beyond the Khyber. By June the situation in Afghanistan had changed largely because of the relief of Jalalabad by the Punjabis. Sher Singh remained a zealous supporter of the British alliance despite the fact that the British harboured his arch enemies, the Sandhawalias.

By the summer of 1842, the rising in Afghanistan had been put down. The scheme of putting Shah Shuja on the throne had proved an expensive failure and was not taken up again. Fortunately for the British, Shah Shuja was killed on 5th April 1842 and they decided to scrap the Tripartite Treaty and make terms with Dost Mohammed. The Amir was released from detention and brought back to Kabul.

The experience of the Afghan campaign soured even the Anglophile Sher Singh. He leant a willing ear to Dhyan Singh Dogra, who pointed out how the British had used the Punjab as a stepping-stone to reach Afghanistan, and having done so, unilaterally abrogated the Tripartite Treaty without consulting the Durbar. The British had also assembled the largest army ever got together by them in India—at Ferozepur only forty miles from Lahore—without explaining the object of the muster. Cunningham wrote: 'Perhaps so many Europeans had never stood together under arms on Indian ground since Alexander and his Greeks made the Punjab a province of Macedon.'

Consequently, when in the winter of 1842 Lord Ellenborough expressed a desire to meet Sher Singh and thank him personally for the part played by the Punjabis in the Afghan campaigns, Sher Singh, who had first agreed to the reception, lost nerve and excused himself on the flimsy ground of protocol. The Governor-General had to content himself with shaking hands with Sher Singh's son, the eleven-year-old Pertap Singh, and Dhyan Singh Dogra. The meeting took place at Ferozepur in January 1843.

It soon transpired that the army collected on the borders of the Punjab was not entirely for display. The defeat in Afghanistan had been a grievous loss of face and the British Government wanted to achieve something spectacular to recover their lost prestige. The choice was between conquering the Punjab or Sindh. Schemes for taking the Punjab had not been finalised and from their performance in Afghanistan, the British had realised that the Punjabis would be a tough nut to crack. So it was decided to take Sindh. Without waiting for an excuse, Sir Charles Napier occupied the province in March 1843. 'The real cause of the chastisement of the Amirs', says Kaye, 'consisted in the chastisement which the British had received from the Afghans. It was deemed expedient at the stage of the great political journey to show that the British could beat someone, and so it was determined to beat the Amirs of Sindh.'

The relationship between the Punjab Government and the British cooled visibly. The Durbar continued to keep up appearances but stopped playing second fiddle to the British. The Punjabis gave Dost Mohammed, who had crossed swords with them in innumerable battles, a great reception when he passed through Lahore on the way to Kabul. The Durbur also entered into a separate agreement with him, recognising him as Amir of Afghanistan.

The British sensed that they had through their maladroitness lost faith with Sher Singh and were not likely to regain it as long as Dhyan Singh Dogra remained the Maharajah's Chief Counsellor. Still persisting in their pretensions of friendship, Clerk put pressure on Sher Singh to allow the Sandhawalia Sardars, Ajit Singh and Attar Singh, who were known to be inimical towards Dhyan Singh Dogra, to return to the Punjab and have their estates and castles restored to them. Sher Singh who had also been irked by the increasing power of the Dogras agreed to the request.

In November 1842, Ajit Singh Sandhawalia arrived at Lahore and was received with open arms by the simple-minded Sher Singh. Lehna Singh was released from prison and the Sandhawalias were reinstated in their possessions. As was perhaps anticipated, the Sandhawalias became the pro-British, anti-Dhyan Singh Dogra party in the Lahore Durbar.

Although Sher Singh befriended Ajit Singh Sandhawalia and the two became boon companions, in matters of policy he continued to accept the guidance of the astute Dhyan Singh Dogra. The arrangement was not to the liking of the Sandhawalias, who were more keen on power than on friendship, nor to the British, who interpreted Dhyan Singh's independent policy as anti-British.

Whether the Sandhawalias acted on their own initiative or on the assurance of support from the British will never be known, for in the holocaust that followed, all possible evidence was washed out in blood. Once more we have an account of the incident from the pen of Dr. Honigberger, who claims to have been 'by accident not farther than ten steps from the place where the horrid crime was committed'.

The 15th September 1843, being the first of the month of *Asuj* by the Hindu calendar, it was arranged that Sher Singh would take the salute at a march past and inspect the troops of Ajit Singh Sandhawalia. The parade was to take place on the open ground near the garden retreat of Shah Bilawal. The night preceding was spent in festivity as Ishar Kaur, the most beautiful of Sher Singh's Maharanis, had given birth to a son. Sher Singh took his elder son Pertap Singh with him and left the child in a neighbouring garden to be weighed against silver which was to be given away in charity. After the march past, the Sandhawalia came up to the platform where the Maharajah was seated to present a double-barrelled gun of English manufacture which he had bought in Calcutta. As the Maharajah extended his arms to receive the weapon, Ajit Singh pressed the trigger. '*Eh ki dagha* (what treachery is this)' exclaimed the unfortunate Maharajah and collapsed where he sat. The Sandhawalia's men fell upon the Maharajah's small escort, while Ajit Singh hacked off the Maharajah's head and mounted it on his spear.

As soon as he heard the gunshot at Shah Bilawal, Lehna Singh Sandhawalia rushed into the neighbouring garden, seized Pertap Singh and ignoring the child's plea for mercy, severed his head from its trunk. He also stuck his victim's head on his spear and joined the nephew. The assassins rode to the city flaunting their gory trophies. They met Dhyan Singh Dogra on the way. He remonstrated with them for killing Pertap Singh. 'What is done cannot be undone. Dalip Singh must now be Maharajah,' replied Ajit Singh, and invited the Dogra to come with them to the fort to make the proclamation. Dhyan Singh had a very small escort and though he became uneasy at the behaviour of the Sandhawalias, he had no option but to accompany them. The party went through the first gate. Then Ajit Singh distracted the Dogra's attention by pointing to some soldiers posted on the ramparts and shot him in the back. 'You murdered my sister-in-law,' he said, referring to the killing of Chand Kaur. The Dogra bodyguard of twenty-five men was hacked to pieces.

Suchet Singh and Hira Singh, who were encamped a couple of miles outside the city, got the news of the murders of the Maharajah and his son. They also received a summons from the Sandhawalias asking them to repair post-haste to the fort. But they were wary and even distrusted the summons bearing the seal of Dhyan Singh. As soon as they got news of Dhyan Singh's murder, they sought refuge with the Khalsa army.

The Sandhawalias occupied the fort and the palace in the belief that they would now rule the Punjab. They had not reckoned with the people.

The news of the dastardly crimes sent a chill of horror through the citizens of Lahore. In the cantonments, the army *Panches* met and resolved to take the city under their protection and to punish the malefactors. They chose as their leader, Hira Singh, the son of Dhyan Singh Dogra, who had appealed to them to help him avenge the murder of his father. He swore that he would go hungry till the Sandhawalias had been punished. Dhyan Singh's widows refused to allow the cremation of their husband's corpse until the heads of the Sandhawalias were placed at its feet. The Dogras harangued the soldiers and told them of the connection between the Sandhawalias and the British. They also offered an increase of another rupee in the monthly pay of the soldiers. The army responded to the appeal and surrounded the fort by evening. All through the night the big guns roared and made several breaches in the wall. Next morning the Nihangs stormed in and captured the citadel.

Hira Singh and his uncle Suchet Singh wreaked terrible vengeance on the Sandhawalias. Ajit Singh was captured trying to escape; Lehna Singh was found hiding in a dungeon with his leg broken. Both the Sardars and six hundred of their troops were put to the sword. Amongst those killed were Bhai Gurmukh Singh and Misr Beli Ram whom Hira Singh Dogra suspected of having beeen inimical towards his father. But Attar Singh Sandhawalia received the news of the death of his kinsmen while he was on his way to Lahore. He also tried to rouse the Sikhs against the Dogras, but his appeal fell on deaf ears. The army, which was largely Sikh, refused to collaborate with a family of regicides. Attar Singh fled across the Sutlej. The British had gained another trump card in their game against the Punjabis.

Dhyan Singh Dogra's limbs, which had been dismembered and thrown in the gutter, were collected. They were put together on the funeral pyre. His widows and maid-servants took their places about the corpse. The chief Rani pinned her husband's aigrette on the turban of Hira Singh and said, 'When I meet your father, I will tell him that you acted as a brave and dutiful son.' The heads of the Sandhawalias were placed at its feet and the dead and living consigned to the flames.

Thus ended the career of Raja Dhyan Singh Dogra, the most controversial character in the history of the Lahore Durbar: by some, including Maharajah Ranjit Singh, considered to be the ablest and most trustworthy of all counsellors; by many others, the evil genius of the Punjab Durbar who was chiefly responsible for the downfall of their kingdom.

Did the British have a hand in the holocaust of the 15th and 16th September 1843? There are a few awkward facts that a British historian would find hard to explain away. The persistence with which Mr. Clerk, the Ludhiana

Agent, pleaded the cause of the Sandhawalias and ultimately persuaded Sher Singh to let them return to Lahore assumes a sinister aspect when we discover that one month before the murder and while the Maharajah was in the best of health, the Governor-General had written: 'The affairs of the Punjab will receive their denouement from the death of Sher Singh.'

The Punjabis believed that the finger on the trigger of the gun which killed Maharajah Sher Singh was that of the British and that they have to answer for the carnage that followed—the murders of the heir-apparent, the Chief Minister and the deaths of over a thousand Punjabi and Dogra soldiers. Even the Anglo-Indian Press of Calcutta admitted that although there was no proof of the East India Company being directly concerned in the murders, it did, in the words of the Journal, *Friend of India*, 'smell a rat'.

Chapter 5

The Punjab under the Dogras

Maharajah Ranjit Singh had many sons but not one of them did he like as much as the precocious and handsome Hira Singh, the son of his Chief Minister Raja Dhyan Singh Dogra. Hira Singh was brought up by the Maharajah like his own child and formally invested with the title, *Farzand-i-Khas* ('Special and Well-Beloved Son'). Ranjit Singh made him a Raja, arranged his marriage, loaded him with rich presents, allowed him the privilege of a seat in Court (a privilege not enjoyed even by the Chief Minister) and the liberty to speak his mind and contradict him. Hira Singh addressed the Maharajah without any formal honorifics, as '*Bapu*' (father). There was little doubt in anyone's mind that if Ranjit Singh had the power to ignore custom and convention, he would have chosen the Dogra boy as his successor. That, however, could not be and Hira Singh had no illusions that the formal ruler of the Punjab had to be a member of the Royal family. But in the atmosphere prevailing at Lahore where the spirit of the late Maharajah still dominated the minds of the Counsellors inasmuch as they tried to make decisions on the principle 'What would have Maharajah Ranjit Singh done under the circumstances?'–it was assumed that Dhyan Singh's place as Chief Minister would be taken by his son Hira Singh.

The matter which agitated the minds of the Durbar was which of his sons should sit on the throne of Ranjit

Singh. The choice fell on the youngest, Dalip Singh, then only six years old. The Sandhawalias had already announced Dalip's accession. Hira Singh also felt that at least during the years of the Prince's minority he would be Chief Minister as well as the *de facto* Maharajah of the Punjab. It is not unlikely that Dalip Singh's mother, the young and beautiful Jindan, who had considerable influence with Hira Singh's uncle, the handsome Suchet Singh Dogra, was able to exert it decisively in favour of her son. Consequently when the corpses were cleared from the streets and peace restored in the city, Dalip Singh was proclaimed Maharajah with Hira Singh Dogra as his Chief Minister.

Neither the blood-letting of the 15th and 16th September nor the proclamation of the new Maharajah lanced the Durbar of its malignant factionalism. There was a realignment of the courtiers behind the claimants to the throne and to the post of Chief Minister. Dalip Singh's pretensions were questioned by his elder stepbrothers, Peshaura Singh and Kashmira Singh. Hira Singh Dogra's chief ministership was questioned by his uncle, Suchet Singh, who was backed by Maharani Jindan (whose lover he was reputed to be), and by his eldest brother Gulab Singh. Since Suchet Singh had no son of his own, Gulab Singh talked him into adopting his (Gulab Singh's) youngest son Ranbir Singh, popularly known as Mian Pheena. This gave Gulab Singh a vested interest in the fortunes of Suchet Singh. Another contender for the post of Chief Minister was Jindan's brother Jawahar Singh, who by virtue of his relationship became a sort of guardian-adviser to the young Maharajah. And yet another character who came on to the Punjab stage as a sort of Chief Minister to the Chief Minister, was a Brahmin priest, Pandit Jalla, who had been companion-tutor to Hira Singh since the latter's childhood. Jalla was an extremely haughty and ill-tempered man and soon came to be disliked by everyone.

The actors on the Durbar stage were, however, soon reduced to mere puppets whose movements were controlled by the army *Panches.* The control was exercised somewhat erratically because the army had no determined policy of its own and apart from forwarding the interests of the men its only other concern was with British designs on the Punjab. The reactions of the men to those suspected of dealing with the British were extremely fierce. The members of the Royal family and the *durbaris* exploited this anglo-phobia of the armed forces in their internal struggles by simply accusing their rivals of being in the pay of the British or, when in trouble themselves, warning the Army of the danger of British invasion. Since the larger part of the defence service was made up of Sikhs, an element of religious fervour came to pervade army circles. A man who came to the fore was one Bhai Bir Singh, a retired soldier who had become an ascetic and set up his own Gurdwara in the village of Naurangabad on the Sutlej.

In times of national crisis, Sikh soldiers and peasantry began to turn to Bhai Bir Singh for guidance. Attending on the Bhai was a volunteer army of 1,200 musketeers and 3,000 horsemen. Over 1,500 pilgrims were fed by his kitchen every day.

The danger of British invasion was no fanciful chimera. There was evidence of military preparations in India and the Punjabis knew that the British only needed an excuse to go to war. British agents were active in the Punjab and had subverted the loyalties of the Durbar's European officers and many of the Sardars. Their tone in dealing with the Punjabis was either patronising or dictatorial. After the murders of Sher Singh and Dhyan Singh, the news of British military preparations and troop movements created a war psychosis in the Punjab.

The Durbar retaliated by spreading disaffection in the Hindusthani regiments of the Company posted on their frontier. Throughout the winter of 1843–44 there were mutinies of sepoys in Sindh and in the cantonments along the Sutlej. In Sindh, the chief cause was the reduction in pay following the annexation of that country and the consequent cancellation of foreign allowance. On the Sutlej, particularly at Ferozepur, they were the result of the disparity between the pay given by the Company (eight and a half rupees per month) and that offered by the Durbar which was twelve and a half rupees per month. Lord Ellenborough was very alarmed at the outbreaks and felt that these mutinies were more dangerous than the hostility of the Khalsa–particularly as he felt that an invasion of the Sutlej would involve an operation of great magnitude and protracted character. The mutinies at Ferozepur became the subject of an acrimonious dispute between the Governor-General and his Commander-in-Chief, as a consequence of which Sir Robert Dick was removed from command on the Sutlej frontier and Major-General Walter Gilbert appointed in his place.

The young Hira Singh Dogra tackled the problems facing him with great energy. He dismissed European officers known to be intriguing with the British and sent spies to find out the military preparations being made across the Sutlej. It was reported that the English had brought more than 200 guns to Ferozepur and were stocking their magazines with powder and ammunition. A European regiment was said to be marching upstream to Rupar. Hira Singh ordered Durbar troops to garrison Kasur (facing Ferozepur) and the moat of Phillaur fort to be flooded with water. In open durbar he asked the British *vakil* to explain why his Government was fortifying Ferozepur and why it had given asylum to Attar Singh Sandhawalia who was known to have been connected with the murders of the previous Maharajah and the Chief Minister and was inimical to the regime of the day. The *vakil* protested the goodwill of the British and said he would convey the Durbar's fears to his Government.

Troop movements on either side of the frontier spread uneasiness in the countryside. The rich began to send their money and jewellery to British India and many families of noblemen fled the Punjab on the pretext of going on pilgrimage to the Ganges. Amongst those who left was Lehna Singh Majithia.

Taking advantage of this state of unrest, Princes Peshaura Singh and Kashmira Singh proclaimed their right to the throne. Hira Singh asked his uncle Gulab Singh Dogra to proceed against the recalcitrant Princes at Sialkot. Gulab Singh undertook the expedition with alacrity as Sialkot adjoined his own territory and would fall into his lap after the Princes had been expelled. Peshaura and Kashmira Singh put up stout resistance and after being ejected from Sialkot toured the Majha country, fraternised with the Sikh peasantry, and then joined Bhai Bir Singh at his camp at Naurangabad. They whipped up anti-Dogra feeling in the army by pointing out that Hira Singh had virtually usurped the throne. The *Panches* called on Hira Singh and demanded, amongst other things, that Dalip Singh should be crowned Maharajah of the Punjab, Peshaura Singh and Kashmira Singh should have their estates restored, and Dogra contingents brought to Lahore should be ordered to return to the hills. Hira Singh agreed to all the demands of the *Panches:* he had learned to say 'yes' to everything without having any intention of doing anything about it. But he was shrewd enough to know that he could not trifle with the army.

The court astrologer, Pandit Madhusudan, fixed 2nd February 1844 as an auspicious day for the coronation and prophesied that the young Maharajah 'would indeed become as great as Alexander.' The Pandit's reckoning of the auspicious day proved as wrong as his prophecy of Dalip's future. On the morning of 2nd February there was a violent hailstorm followed by a heavy downpour which made the coronation a damp and chill affair. Rani Jindan was indignant. A week later, she took her son to Amritsar, had him baptised as a Khalsa and another investiture carried out by Sikh rites. The Maharajah's uncle, Jawahar Singh, who had been imprisoned by the order of Hira Singh, was released. Kashmira Singh and Peshaura Singh had their estates confirmed and were received in the durbar with the honour due to Princes of royal blood.

The next challenge to Hira Singh's stewardship came from his uncle, Suchet Singh Dogra, who believed that Rani Jindan and her brother, Jawahar Singh, would manage a palace revolution for him. Suchet Singh and his lieutenant, Rai Kesri Singh, turned up at Lahore with a small escort of forty-five Dogras and asked the Khasla Army to dismiss Hira Singh and Pandit Jalla.

Hira Singh rose to the crisis. He went to the barracks and pleaded with the men. He asked to be forgiven his trespasses, protested his devotion to the Khalsa and hinted that he might accept baptism in the near future. He convinced the *Panches* that a victory for Suchet Singh would be a triumph of pro-British elements in the Durbar as Suchet Singh had invested large sums of money in the British enterprise in Afghanistan and had been in friendly intercourse with the Sandhawalias when they were in British territory. He said:

'Khalsa ji! The son of your old minister and the adopted son of your old Maharajah now stands in your presence as a suppliant. Tell him, I beg of you, what fault he has committed, to punish which, you have invited his uncle, his greatest enemy and your own inveterate foe, being, as you are aware, a staunch ally of the *feringhi*. If you want to kill me, here is the sword, and I give you full liberty at once to sever my head from my body. It would be an honour for me to die at the hands of the brave Khalsa. But, for the Guru's sake, do not allow me to suffer a death of shame. If you have not called my uncle from the hills, and are not disposed to help him, support me and fight for my cause as good and brave soldiers, and you will receive the blessings of the Guru.'

Hira Singh supplemented his passionate harangue with promises of reward. He gave a gold *butki* worth Rs. 5 to each soldier and a gold necklace to every officer. The Khalsa soldiers went over to his side.

Infantry and cavalry units with 56 guns marched out and surrounded Suchet Singh and his forty-five Dogras at the mausoleum of Mian Wadda not far from the city; The Dogras made a heroic stand. Suchet Singh sat impassively, listening to a recitation of the *Gita* while the Durbar's cannon blasted the walls of the mosque and mausoleum; his men went out in turns to cross swords with the assailants. When most of his companions had fallen, Suchet Singh himself went out. He railed his attackers: 'Relying on your good faith, I came to Lahore at your special invitation. You have forsaken me and have now come to kill me in such numbers. I beseech you at this moment to behave with me like true soldiers. Come on, my friends, come on, one by one, and let the world see the worth of a Rajput soldier.'

Both Suchet Singh and his lieutenant, Rai Kesri Singh, fell fighting to the last. This was on 27th March 1844.

Hira Singh visited the mausoleum soon after the action was over. Kesri Singh, who was still alive, greeted the young minister with '*Jai Dev*' and asked for water. 'The water of the Jammu hills is clear and cool,' replied Hira Singh sarcastically, 'you will soon get it.' But when he saw his uncle's corpse riddled with bullets and covered with sabre wounds, he broke down and cried. The Dogras were given an honourable funeral at Lahore.

Hira Singh did not gain anything by the death of Suchet Singh. Gulab Singh assumed all the deceased's estates in the name of his son Ranbir Singh (adopted by Suchet) and refused to consider Hira Singh's claim to an equal share. A substantial portion of Suchet Singh's treasure, which was in British territory, was attached by the Agent to be subjected to a judicial enquiry. The Army felt that it had been misused by the Dogras to settle a private quarrel. Tension between Sikhs and Dogras mounted and many Sikh soldiers went over to Bhai Bir Singh's purely Sikh camp.

On 9th April 1844, Lahore and Amritsar were shaken by a severe earthquake. To superstitious people this forbode evil days to come. On Baisakhi, which fell two days later, the bazars of Amritsar which were normally festooned for the occasion, remained closed for fear of riots. Instead, the people flocked in their thousands to the camp of Bir Singh and heard the Bhai's sermon on the vanishing glory of Ranjit Singh's Empire.

Durbar circles were far removed from the grim realities of the mounting crisis. On 18th April the palace cat had a litter of kittens and the infant Maharajah desired that a salute should be fired in honour of the occasion. The Chief Minister thereupon ordered miniature guns to be discharged to announce the feline nativity to the citizens of Lahore.

Rumours of an impending war continued to spread. The British were reported to be massing a large army in the Simla Hills to invade the Punjab. Intelligence reports of April 1844 stated that Attar Singh Sandhawalia, who was living in Thanesar in British territory, was in regular communication with Bhai Bir Singh and was contemplating an attack on Lahore. The Durbar army was ordered to keep a watch on the fords and ferries and prevent the Sandhawalia from coming in. But in May, the Sardar managed to elude the Durbar's sentries, crossed the Sutlej and joined the Bhai's camp at Naurangabad, He was welcomed by the Bhai with the words: 'The throne of the Punjab awaits you.'

The Governor-General, Lord Ellenborough, admitted that the British were at fault in letting Attar Singh cross over into Sikh territory. In a letter to Queen Victoria dated 10th June 1844 he wrote: 'It is much to be regretted that Attar Singh should have been permitted to move from Thanesar to the Sutlej with the known object of acting against the Lahore Government. This error of the British

Agent renders it impossible to protest against the violation of the strict letter of the treaty which was committed by the Sikhs, whose troops were sent to the left bank to intercept Attar Singh and, under all the circumstances, it has been deemed expedient to make no representation upon the subject, but to allow the whole matter to be forgotten.'

Princes Kashmira Singh and Peshaura Singh also left Sialkot and came to Bhai Bir Singh's camp. They promised to support Attar Singh Sandhawalia. Amongst the Sardars known to be in communication with the Bhai were Sham Singh Attariwala, Lehna Singh Majithia and Jemadar Khushal Singh. Naurangabad thus became the centre of a Sikh revolt against the Dogra-dominated Lahore Court.

Hira Singh Dogra again harangued the soldiers and told them that the Sandhawalia's hands were soiled with blood; that he had been with the English for the last six months and had promised to give the British six annas of each rupee collected in revenue if his venture succeeded; that Suchet Singh's widow had undertaken to finance the revolt from the money her husband had invested in British India; and that Bhai Bir Singh and the Princes had unwittingly become tools in the hands of traitors. The *Panches* agreed to side with Hira Singh and Durbar troops marched out to Naurangabad. They were commanded by a Dogra Officer, Mian Labh Singh.

Prince Peshaura Singh left the Bhai's camp and made his submission to the Durbar. A little later, he left the Punjab and sought asylum with the British.

Bhai Bir Singh's efforts were now directed to bringing about an amicable settlement between the Durbar and the two men who had sought shelter with him; Attar Singh Sandhawalia and Prince Kashmira Singh. He invited the Durbar's troops to be his guests and slaughtered five hundred goats to feed them. The Bhai's attempt at conciliation was undone by Attar Singh Sandhawalia, who lost his temper and killed one of the Durbar's emissaries, Gulab Singh Kalkattea. Durbar artillery opened fire and blasted the Bhai's camp, killing six hundred men, including Attar Singh Sandhawalia and Prince Kashmira Singh. A cannon-ball broke Bir Singh's thigh.

Before he died, the Bhai spoke to the Sikh officers who had written to him asking him to support Attar Singh. 'When you and your chiefs and officers wrote these letters to me, with the most solemn promises, both to myself and Attar Singh, I relied on your good faith, and agreed to your proposals, in the hope of obtaining for Attar Singh and his family the means of a quiet livelihood. You have proved yourselves a vile, treacherous and unfaithful race, without pity or religion. Still, my dying prayer to heaven is, may even your wickedness be requited by good.' Bir Singh asked that his corpse be thrown in the Sutlej and died with a curse on his lips. 'Let not my body rot in this land of iniquity . . .'

The Khalsa soldiers were filled with remorse when they discovered that they had killed a large number of men, women and children. General Court's battalion, which had taken the leading part in the fighting, was promptly doubed *Gurumar*–killers of the Guru. Mian Labh Singh further exasperated the Sikhs by arresting Rani Daya Kaur, widow of Maharajah Ranjit Singh and the mother of Princes Kashmira Singh and Peshaura Singh. Troopers shot the Dogra Colonel put in charge of the Rani and liberated her. The men clamoured for vengeance. Mian Labh Singh had to flee for his life.

Hira Singh realised that the killing of Bir Singh had aroused violent passions. He gave Rs. 5,000 for *Karah Pershad* in memory of the Bhai and proclaimed his intentions of accepting baptism to the Khalsa fraternity. The *Punjab News Letter* of 14th May 1844 reported that 'Raja Hira Singh endeavours to keep the soldiers in good humour.' The Sikh soldiers took the gifts but said, 'We killed our Guru and we get two rupees, what sort of men are we?'

Once more extraneous events came to Hira Singh's rescue and he was able to avert destruction at the hands of the soldiers. Maharajah Dalip Singh contracted small-pox and was reported to be dying. The people did not want another violent change in the administration while the very existence of the State was in jeopardy. The British were said to be laying in more supplies in their cantonments and examining the fords over which they would cross the Sutlej. The newswriter from Kasauli reported that large quantities of ammunition had been forwarded to Ludhiana and Ferozepur. Reports from Ferozepur said that zamindars had been advised not to sow an autumn crop as a very large army was to assemble there.

Although the immediate crisis was averted, communal tension continued to mount. The Sikhs now focussed their hatred on the Brahmin Pandit, Jalla. On 22nd June 1844, there was a stormy scene in the durbar when Hira Singh Dogra reprimanded Attar Singh Kalianwala for rudeness to Jalla: the Sardar had only taken his seat next to the Pandit. All the Sikh Sardars, including Bhaia Ram Singh and Sham Singh Attariwala left the court with loud cries of '*Wah Guru ji ka Khalsa, Wah Guru ji ka Fateh*'. Later a conspiracy to murder Hira Singh Dogra and Pandit Jalla was unearthed. Amongst the Chiefs concerned was Sham Singh Attariwala.

Disloyal elements took advantage of Hira Singh's discomfiture. In the South, Fathe Khan Tiwana shook off allegiance to the Punjab Government. Julraj, son of Dewan Sawan Mal, Governor of Multan, was sent against him. An action was fought at Mitha Tiwana on 17th June 1844 in which nine hundred men were killed on both sides, one of the casualties being Fateh Khan's son. Tiwana submitted and asked to be forgiven. Then Gulab Singh Dogra, who had already proclaimed the seizure of all Suchet Singh's property, refused to send revenue to Lahore.

Pandit Jalla urged the Durbar to take action against Gulab Singh Dogra as it had taken action against Fateh Khan Tiwana. Gulab Singh countered the move by offering to pay if the Pandit was handed over to him; he had gallows put up in Jammu to tell the people what he intended to do to Jalla. The *Panches* were reluctant to commit the army in what they believed was a private feud between the Dogras. Hira Singh tried to convince them that his uncle was in league with the British. Gulab Singh incited the frontier tribesmen to revolt against the Durbar and plunder Peshawar. This act of disloyalty convinced the *Panches* that there was substance in Hira Singh's allegations and they used their influence to get the army to march on to Jammu. Gulab Singh submitted without a fight and made peace with his nephew by sending his son Sohan Singh as hostage to Lahore.

In July 1844, Lord Ellenborough was replaced by Sir Henry Hardinge. The appointment of the *tunda lat* (the one-armed Lord), who was a distinguished soldier, as Governor-General caused nervousness in Durbar circles. When the news was read out in court, Pandit Jalla remarked; 'Lord Auckland had crushed Afghans and his successor, Lord Ellenbrough, had invaded Sindh and Gwalior and now the new Lord was no doubt, willing to invade the Punjab.' The remarks were occasioned by the information received a week earlier that the Council at Calcutta had, at its secret sitting, regretted the death of Attar Singh Sandhawalia because, if he had lived, the British would have acquired the Punjab without a fight. Deserters from the Company's forces said that the British planned to cross the Sutlej in September. September passed without any incident but when the Commander-in-Chief of the Company's forces came up to inspect the British troops at Ludhiana and Ferozepur in October, the Punjab army was alerted against a possible invasion. Frontier outposts on the river were quickly garrisoned and a twenty-four-hour watch kept on the opposite bank.

The British did not invade the Punjab that autumn, and after a few weeks the tension eased. The Punjab army returned to the cantonments at Lahore and was quickly involved in Court intrigues. The relationship between the Sikhs and Dogras became tense again. This time it was caused by Pandit Jalla's reflections on Rani Jindan's character. The Rani's name had been linked with many courtiers, the latest being Misr Lal Singh by whom she was reported to have become pregnant. The pregnancy was aborted but the Rani became very ill. It was said in open court that if Jindan died, Lal Singh would be executed. Jindan, however, survived the operation. She sent for her brother Jawahar Singh from Amritsar. The Rani and her brother took Dalip Singh with an escort of Ventura's dragoons to the cantonment. In an impassioned speech the Rani asked the soldiers to choose between her son, Maharajah Dalip Singh, and the Dogra-Jalla regime. The soldiers were incensed against Hira Singh because only a day earlier he had dismissed five hundred of their comrades and confiscated their pay. They acclaimed Jindan and her son, and swore to drive Hira Singh and Jalla out of the Punjab.

Hira Singh, realising his precarious position, turned to his uncle for help. Gulab singh hurried down from

Jammu with 1,000 Dogras. The news of the descent of the hillmen precipitated matters and the army clamoured for blood. Hira Singh and Jalla came out of the fort on the pretence of going to the cantonment to talk to the *Panches*, but suddenly turned from their course and crossed the Ravi to Shahdara; with them were a couple of thousand Dogras and several elephant-, horse-, and cart-loads of treasure. A detachment of Durbar troops went in hot pursuit.

The Durbar troops caught up with the fleeing Dogra and his mentor, fourteen miles from Lahore and a running battle commenced between the two forces. Amongst the earliest casualties was Pandit Jalla, who fell off his horse from physical exhaustion and was cut down by the pursuers. Mian Labh Singh made a rearguard stand in the hope that his master would be able to join the Dogras coming to his rescue. The Durbar troops did not lose much time in disposing of Mian Labh Singh and again caught up with Hira Singh who had entrenched himself in a village. The pursuers set fire to the village and forced the hillmen out in the open. Over one thousand Dogras perished in the fight. The heads of Hira Singh, Jalla, Mian Labh Singh and Sohan Singh (son of Gulab Singh) were impaled on spears and paraded through the streets of Lahore. This took place on 21st December 1844.

Hira Singh Dogra, like his eminent father, was a very controversial figure. According to Col. Gardner, he was 'crouching and mean to his superiors; silent and suspicious with his equals; proud, supercilious, and arrogant to his inferiors; subtle and deceitful to all. Too much puffed up to return or even notice the salutations of better men than himself; reared as the lapdog of Ranjit Singh and his dissolute companions; with a smattering of English, Persian and Sanskrit, and pretending to a perfect knowledge of all three languages.' That is, however, not the impression one gets from his conduct of affairs. On the contrary, he appears to have been endowed with talent, tact and courage. If circumstances had been different, he might well have become the first Dogra-Sikh Maharajah of Lahore. Hira Singh's memory is preserved by the locality where he lived, being named after him as *Hira Mandi.* During British rule this became the prostitute quarter of the city. But it was Pandit Jalla, the *éminence grise* of the Durbar, who led to the downfall of Hira Singh. Jalla's memory came to be execrated:

> *Upper Allah, Talley Jalla.*
> *Jalley dey sir tey khalla.*
> (In Heaven there is Allah, On earth there is Jalla. May He smack Jalla on the head with a shoe.)

Jalla's name, however, was immortalised. A squarish plot of open land that the Pandit owned in the heart of Amritsar came to be known after him as Jallianwala Bagh. Seventy-five years after Jalla's death, the citizens of Amritsar gathered in this garden named after him in defiance of an order prohibiting all meetings. General Dyer dispersed the gathering with machine gun fire, killing over three hundred unarmed men, women and children. The massacre of Jallianwala Bagh was the decisive turning point in the history of India's freedom movement because it turned the masses irrevocably against the British.

Chapter 6

British Plans to Annex the Punjab

The series of blood baths left the Durbar in a state of utter exhaustion. Many princes of royal blood and contenders for a ministerial power had been murdered; some, like Lehna Singh Majithia, had fled the State, or like Fakir Azizuddin had chosen to live in comparative obscurity rather than gamble with their lives. It seemed that every one had had enough and Rani Jindan and her brother, Jawahar Singh, would be given a chance to restore the rule of law in the name of the infant King, Dalip Singh. But that was not to be so, as by then the British were ready with their plans of annexation and it was in their interest to keep the Punjab administration unstable.

The blueprint of the invasion was prepared early in 1844. The arrival of Sir Henry Hardinge in July once again heated up the cold war which had been going on for some time. Hardinge brought his two sons with him to handle his secret correspondence. This correspondence reveals the methodical way in which aggression against the Punjab was planned and how men and munitions were moved up to their allotted places on the frontier in time for the campaigning season which began in the autumn. On 17th September Sir Henry Hardinge wrote to Ellenborough: 'On the north-west frontier, I am in correspondence with Gough to get all our troops of horse artillery and bullocks in complete order; and we propose to send our companies of Europeans, picked men, to fill up vacancies.'

New barracks were built to house the troops. Broadfoot, whose name stank in the nostrils of the Punjabis and who had the reputation of being 'rather too prone to war', was nominated to replace Col. Richmond as British Agent at Ludhiana.

The first thing Broadfoot did was to proclaim that Durbar possessions on the eastern bank of the Sutlej would be treated exactly as the possessions of the protected Chiefs of Malwa and subject to escheat on the extinction of the line of succession. The proclamation was made at a time when Dalip Singh was down with small-pox and not expected to live. The Durbar took a serious view of this decision and considered it to be a contravention of the Treaty of 1809 and the subsequent agreements, particularly regarding Annandpur and Kot Kapura near Ferozepur. To the people who did not understand legal niceties, it meant that the British had annexed the Durbar's cis-Sutlej territories as the first step towards the annexation of the rest of the Punjab.

An incident which took place in March 1845 showed the temper of men like Broadfoot. One Lal Singh *Adalti*, a magistrate in the service of the Durbar, crossed the Sutlej into Durbar territory in connection with his official work. Broadfoot, who happened to be in the vicinity, not only ordered *Adalti's* party to turn back at once, but while they were getting into their boats, captured some of them and fired on others. Even Broad-foot was hard put to explain the arrest of a Lahore Judge on Lahore soil. The shot fired on this occasion was described by Campbell in his Memoirs as the 'first shot of the Great Sikh War'. Broadfoot's aggressive behaviour led Cunningham to record: 'It was generally held by the English in India that Major Broadfoot's appointment greatly increased the probabilities of a war with the Sikhs, and the impression was equally strong that had Mr. Clerk, for instance, not been removed as Agent, there would have been no war.'

The murders of Hira Singh Dogra and Pandit Jalla gave the annexation project a sense of urgency. The British decided to keep the Punjab pot on the boil till they had assembled their forces.

Prince Peshaura Singh, who had been living in British territory, was allowed to return to the Punjab to stake his claim against Dalip Singh. The situation at Lahore deteriorated even more rapidly than Broadfoot had envisaged. The Company's forces were however, far from ready for a major campaign and the winter season, during which they preferred to do their fighting, was half over. In a letter dated 23rd January 1845, Hardinge apprised Ellenbourough of the state of affairs. He wrote: 'Even if we had a case for devouring our ally in adversity, we are not ready . . . moderation will do us no harm, if in the interval the hills and the plains weaken each other; but on what plea could we attack the Punjab if this were the month of October, and we had our army in readiness?' The letter continues: 'Self-preservation may require the dispersion of the Sikh army, the baneful influence of such an example is the evil most to be dreaded. But exclusive of this case, how are we to justify the seizure of our friend's territory who in our adversity assisted us to retrieve our affairs?'

The hills and the plains had begun to weaken each other almost as if to facilitate a British invasion. Gulab Singh Dogra once again defied the authority of the Durbar and in February 1845, troops had to be withdrawn from their defensive posts along the Sutlej and directed towards Jammu. The leaders of the expedition were Sham Singh Attariwala, Mewa Singh Majithia, Sultan Mahmud Khan and Fateh Singh Man. The few skirmishes the Dogras had with the Punjabi plainsmen convinced them that they could not win in a fair fight. Gulab Singh turned to duplicity. He came to the Punjabi camp with a very small escort and put his sword and shield at the feet of the Army *Panches.* He recapitulated the services he had rendered to Ranjit Singh and the Sikhs. Words of flattery were accompanied by lavish gifts of gold and silver and four lakhs of rupees were handed over in cash as tribute to the Durbar. The *Panches* forgave the Dogra and the Generals ordered the troops back to Lahore. They had not got very far from Jammu when they were ambushed and Fateh Singh Man and his chief aide, Wazir Bachna, were killed. The pack animals carrying the tribute were driven away–presumably back to Gulab Singh's treasury.

The *Panches* rushed their men back to Jammu. After an initial setback, Sham Singh Attariwala and Ranjodh Singh Majithia inflicted a severe defeat on the Dogras. Gulab Singh again made his submission. He came to the Sikh camp 'with his hands folded and a sheet thrown round his neck as a suppliant' and asked to be punished for his sins. He swore that he had nothing to do with the ambush, the killing of Fateh Singh Man or the looting of the treasury. The *Panches* again accepted Gulab Singh's explanations and made peace with him. It was said that Gulab Singh gave a gold ring to each soldier and another 3 lakhs in cash to the Durbar. Officers and troops were lavishly entertained with wine and courtesans. Success emboldened Gulab Singh. He spoke to the men of the way Rani Jindan and her brother Jawahar Singh conducted themselves—particularly of the way they had allowed a maid-servant, Mangla, the daughter of a *jheevar* (water carrier) to become the go-between Jindan and Raja Lal Singh and herself became the mistress of Jawahar Singh. Gulab Singh convinced the army that it would be better for the Punjab to have Prince Peshaura Singh as Maharajah rather than Dalip Singh, and he, Gulab Singh Dogra, as Chief Minister, instead of Jawahar Singh or the Rani's paramour Lal Singh. The *Panches* could not make up their minds and decided to bring Gulab Singh Dogra to Lahore—a captive who could also be King-maker.

Gulab Singh was well received in the Durbar. He stayed in the capital for three months sowing as much dissension as he could, His star, however, remained in the descendant. He had to accept the confirmation of Jawahar Singh as Chief Minister and suffer the rise of the Attariwala family to supreme importance by virtue of the betrothal of Chattar Singh's daughter to Maharajah Dalip Singh. Jawahar Singh used his influence to penalise the Dogra. Gulab Singh was fined Rs 68 lakhs, ordered to hand over the estates of his brother Suchet Singh and nephew Hira Singh and the lease of the salt mines was renewed at a very much higher rate than before. Gulab Singh suffered his wings to be clipped in the knowledge that if he protested too much he might lose his life in the same way as other members of his family had lost theirs. He returned to Jammu shorn of some of his wealth but determined to teach the Durbar a lesson, even if it involved dealing with the English.

While the pick of the Durbar's army was engaged in the hills, the plains and the cities of Amritsar and Lahore were practically undefended, Lord Hardinge speeded up the troop movements. 'We shall now begin to move up the additional regiments to Ferozepur, Ludhiana and Ambala, the barracks etc. being nearly ready,' he wrote to Ellenborough on 8th March 1845. 'As the fords deepen and the heat increases, these movements will cause no alarm; but quietly we will get the troops in their proper place.' A fleet of flat-bottomed boats was assembled on the eastern bank of the Sutlej to form a pontoon bridge. By the middle of the summer of 1845 the boats were ready to be put in operation. Charles Hardinge, who was acting Secretary to his father, wrote to the Agent at Ludhiana explaining their purport: 'They are of equal dimensions, each carrying a gun, two grappling irons with strong chains, and 100 men; the 60 boats would, therefore, for short distances, such as the passage of a river, carry 6,000 infantry at one trip.' The young subaltern added words of advice to the seasoned intriguer: 'It is not desirable that the purposes to which these boats can be applied should unnecessarily transpire.' If questioned by the *vakil* of the Lahore Durbar, Broadfoot was to state that they were to be used to meet the increase of mercantile traffic on the Indus.

Another incident, this time on the southern frontier, confirmed the Durbar's fears of English intentions towards the Punjab. A party of Durbar horsemen, who had gone in pursuit of raiders, crossed into the noman's land between the undefined frontiers of the Punjab and the newly annexed province of Sindh. Sir Charles Napier utilised this as an excuse and ordered a whole regiment to march towards the frontier at Rojhan.

There were many things besides the summer season which made the British hold their hand till the autumn. Durbar troops had returned from the Jammu front and it was felt that a larger force than the one assembled on the frontier would be needed for the operation. The higher pay offered by the Durbar had induced many sepoys of the Company to desert; there had been more mutinies among the Company's Indian troops which the Commander-in-Chief, Lord Gough, had to suppress with force: he reintroduced flogging as a punishment. Although the trouble was suppressed, English officers did not have the necessary confidence in their Hindustani sepoys. In May, Broadfoot, who was the chief architect of the projected annexation, was taken ill and had to be removed to Simla.

While convalescing, he fell from his horse and was put out of action for another couple of months. In June, an epidemic of cholera broke out at Lahore and rapidly spread all over the province (amongst those afflicted were Sham Singh Attariwala and Lal Singh). By July, the epidemic had spread across the Sutlej to the British cantomments in Ferozepur and Ludhiana. When the epidemic subsided, there were disturbances on the frontier caused by rival Sodhi factions at Annandpur. Another thing which made the Governor-General hold his hand was the presence of Mohan Lal Kashmiri in London. This man had been attached as Persian translator to Sir Alexander Burnes and had gone to England in connection with the probate of his late employer's will. His special knowledge of the Afghan campaign and the state of the Punjab made him a much sought-after figure in the British capital. He was invited to speak at meetings; statesmen asked his advice; publishers commissioned him to write of his travels in the Punjab and the life of Dost Mohammed of Afghanistan. Mohan Lal warned his audiences of the danger of adopting an aggressive attitude towards the Punjabis. As Hardinge had intended to break the news of Sikh 'aggression' he had to wait till he knew the reaction to Mohan Lal's speeches in the circles that mattered. Besides these extraneous factors, was the practical one of the military strength of the Durbar and its capacity of gaining allies for its defence. The only people to whom the Punjabis could now turn for aid to repel aggression were the Pathans and the Afghans. British agents got to know that the Durbar had opened negotiations with Sultan Mohammed Khan Barakzai, brother of Amir Dost Mohammed, on the basis of the transfer of Peshawar District to him in lieu of help against the British. British policy till then was either to have a subservient Punjab or to annex it outright rather than suffer it to become a Muslim State. The following two letters are illuminating. On 19th January 1845, Sir Frederick Currie wrote to Broadfoot: 'I imagine we shall be forced to cross the Sutlej sooner or later, and you will see we are sending troops to be ready for whatever may turn up. We must not have a Mohammedan power on this side of the Attock. The Rajputs of the Hills could not hold the Punjab, and if it cannot be Sikh, it must, I suppose, be British.'

On 4th October 1845, Broadfoot wrote to Hardinge: 'A vigorous effort will be made to accomplish it (i.e., the transfer of Peshwar to the Afghans) before we invade or at least before we conquer, in order that it may be for us *fait accompli* . . . I agree with you that for us to suffer a Barakzai power at Peshawar, with us at Lahore, would be most impolitic.'

In view of all these difficulties, the invasion had to be postponed. Meanwhile, military preparations were kept up and manoeuvres to undermine the authority of the Durbar continued unabated. A ready pawn was Prince Peshaura Singh who, as has already been stated, had been welcomed back to the Punjab.

On the night of 14th July 1845, Prince Peshaura Singh led a band of seven desperadoes into the fort of Attock and bluffed its entire garrison into laying down their arms. From Attock, he proclaimed his accession to the throne and exhorted the peasants of the neighbouring country to declare their allegiance to him. He opened negotiations with the Barakzais and also offered them Peshawar in exchange for help in taking Lahore. The story of the way the Prince seized Attock made him into a hero. 'True son of Ranjit Singh,' said the peasants and the soldiers. Courtiers found another trump card to play against the triumvirate of Jindan, Jawahar Singh and Dalip Singh. Gulab Singh Dogra utilised the situation to secure permission to return to Jammu.

The troops sent out to crush the revolt were not only reluctant to fight but were inclined to bring the Prince to Lahore to replace Dalip Singh and the coterie which surrounded him. The commanders of the punitive expedition, Chattar Singh Attariwala and Fateh Khan Tiwana, pretended to share the sentiments of the troops and pleaded with Peshaura Singh not to fight them. The Prince accepted the assurances given to him and evacuated the fort. The Lahore force greeted the Prince with a salute of guns and both Attariwala and Tiwana paid their homage to him. The convoy started on its way back to the capital.

Twenty miles from Attock Peshaura Singh agreed to break journey to hunt for wild pig which abounded in the country; the troops were ordered to continue their march homewards. When the Prince was without his personal bodyguard and was relaxing after a strenuous morning of pig-sticking, he was seized and taken back to Attock. He was strangled to death, and his limbs cut up and thrown in the Indus that ran below the ramparts. Chattar Singh Attariwala made his way towards the Jammu hills; Fateh Khan Tiwana went to Dera Ismail Khan. These men had connived at the murder of prince Peshaura Singh and were handsomely rewarded by Wazir Jawahar Singh. The Army had once again been duped and made an instrument of intrigue by factions in the Durbar.

When the news of the murder of Prince Peshaura Singh spread, the citizens and soldiers were in a very dark mood. The *Panches* deliberated in the cantonment at Mian Mir and after prolonged discussion decided that the Army should take over the administration. The *Panches* began to issue orders in the name of the Khalsa Panth under the seal *Akhal Sahai*–'the Lord is our helper'. They ordered Jawahar Singh, Rani Jindan and Dalip Singh to appear before an army tribunal and explain the death of Prince Peshaura Singh.

Jawahar Singh ignored the summons. He had the gates of the fort shut and posted Col. Gardner's battalion inside to guard the palace. The troops surrounded the fort and asked the minister to submit to the orders of the *Panchayat*.

Rani Jindan tried to win over the men by appealing to their sense of patriotism. The British, she said, were on the banks of the Sutlej ready to invade their country. She sent Fakir Nuruddin, Dina Nath and Attar Singh Kalianwala to plead with the men. The *Panches* detained two of the emissaries and sent the Fakir back with the message that if the gates were not opened within twenty-four hours and Jawahar Singh handed over for trial, the artillery would blast them with gunfire. Jawahar Singh made a desperate attempt to evade justice. He offered a bribe of Rs. 50,000 to the guards to let him escape. An officer took the bribe; a common soldier refused and promptly arrested Jawahar Singh in the name of the Khalsa Panth.

Lt. Col. Gardner, who was an eye-witness, described the scene that followed in dramatic detail:

'On September 21, 1845, Jawahir Singh was summoned before the army. He came out on an elephant, holding in his arms his nephew, the young Maharajah Dhulip Singh, the last survivor of the line of Ranjit Singh. The Maharani Jindan accompanied him on another elephant. Jawahir Singh had an escort of 400 horsemen, and two elephant-loads of rupees with which to tempt the army. As soon as the cavalcade left the fort an ominous salute ran along the immense line of the army—180 guns were fired. A roll-call was beat, and not a man of that great host was absent. So terribly stern was their discipline that, after the salute had died away, not a sound was to be heard but the trampling of the feet of the royal cavalcade.

'Dhulip Singh was received with royal honours: his mother, the Maharani Jindan, in miserable terror for her brother, was seated on her golden *hauda,* dressed in white Sikh clothes and closely veiled. As soon as the procession reached the middle of the line one man came forward and cried out, "Stop", and at his single voice the whole procession paused. A tremor ran through the host: many expected a rescue on the part of the French brigade; but not a man stirred. The great *Panch* (Military Council) was still sitting on the right of the line. Four battalions were now ordered to the front, and removed Jawahir Singh's escort to a distance. Then another battalion marched up and surrounded the elephants of the royal personages. Ten of the Council then came forward; the Rani's elephant was ordered to kneel down, and she herself was escorted to a small but beautiful tent prepared for her close by.

'Then a terrible scene took place. The Rani was dragged away, shrieking to the army to spare her brother. Jawahir Singh was next ordered to descend from his elephant. He lost his head, attempted to parley and a tall Sikh slapped his face and took the boy Dhulip Singh, from his arms, asking him how he dared to disobey the Khalsa. Dhulip Singh was placed in his mother's arms, and she, hiding herself behind the walls of her tent held the child up above them in view of the army, crying for mercy for her brother in the name of her son. Suddenly, hearing a yell of agony from a well-known voice, she flung the child away in an agony of grief and rage. Fortunately, he was caught by a soldier, or the consequences might have been fatal.

'Meanwhile the bloody work had been done on the hated minister. A soldier who had presumably received his orders, had gone up the ladder placed by Jawahar Singh's elephant, stabbed him with his bayonet, and flung him upon the ground, where he was dispatched in a moment with fifty wounds.

'Thus did the Sikh army avenge the death of Kashmira Singh and Peshora Singh.'

The *Panches* deliberated all through the night with Jindan and Jawahar Singh's widows wailing in the background. Common soldiers taunted them: 'Now you know what Peshaura Singh's mother felt when you had the Prince murdered.' Jindan threatened to immolate herself and her son Maharajah Dalip Singh on Jawahar Singh's funeral pyre. Her lamentations moved the soft-hearted *Panches.* Dina Nath and Attar Singh Kalianwala were released to dissuade her from committing suicide. Jawahar Singh's body was taken back to the fort and later in the morning cremated with four of his wives committing *sati* on the pyre. Thus ended the last of the sanguinary episodes in the Lahore Durbar.

The *Panches* met again in the afternoon to determine ways and means of running the administration. They were peasants with no knowledge of administrative procedure or the niceties of diplomatic usage. Consequently they decided that although matters of fundamental policy should be determined by them, the details of their execution should be handled by ministers whom they could trust. Dewan Dina Nath and Fakir Azizuddin were the two men whose integrity could not be impugned. The Fakir was anxious to withdraw from active life, particularly as he disapproved of the measures being taken against the English. The choice therefore fell on Dina Nath, whose first job was to announce the execution of Jawahar Singh. Dalip Singh was to continue nominally as the Maharajah of the Punjab with his mother Rani Jindan as Regent. But neither of them nor any of the ministers were to be allowed to communicate with any foreign power—particularly the British—without the prior sanction of the Army *Panchayat*. An official communique was sent to the British Government stating that the Khalsa Panth wanted peace, but if the British continued to march troops to Ludhiana and Ferozepur, it would be compelled to safeguard its frontiers; and if the British invaded the Punjab, the Punjabis would fight and expel them. It ended by exhorting the British not to make preparations for war and to avoid creating an atmosphere of hostility.

A week after the execution of Jawahar Singh on 27th September 1854, an oath of allegiance to Dalip Singh and Jindan was taken by the soldiers at all regimental centres. They swore to fight the *feringhi*, if necessary across the Sutlej. The Durbar moved to Amritsar for Dussehra—the festival was celebrated with parades, mock-battles and the worship of arms. Here once more Sikh soldiers flocked to the Golden Temple to pray for victory against the foreigner.

On its way back, the Durbar halted for a few days at the Shalamar Gardens where a most dramatic meeting took place. Dewan Dina Nath surveyed the events of the past months and read letters from officers posted in the Durbar's territories across the Sutlej stating that the British were demanding tributes from them as if the territories had already been annexed. He made special reference to Annandpur, the holy town of Gurus Tegh

Bahadur and Gobind Singh. He warned the *Panches* and the ministers that if the administration of the State was allowed to deteriorate further and dissension in Durbar circles continued, the kingdom of Ranjit Singh would fall an easy prey to the aggressor. The Dewan's address created a profound impression on his audience. The *Panches* resolved to choose leaders at once. At the Dewan's suggestion (at the instance of Jindan) they accepted Lal Singh as Chief Minister and Tej Singh as Commander-in-Chief. The nominations were confirmed at a formal ceremony at the mausoleum of Ranjit Singh where the *Panches* and officers again took the oath of loyalty to the State.

Col. Gardner gives an idea of the atmosphere in the Punjab. He says that such was 'the real belief that the intentions of the British were aggressive, such the domestic incitements of their families to plunder, and such their devotion to their mystic faith, that one single dogged determination filled the bosom of each soldier. The word went round, "We will go to the sacrifice." One miserable deserter was nearly beaten to death by his Punjabi countrywomen.'

Chapter 7

First War against the English

The threat of invasion from the East brought the nation together. Self-seeking courtiers of the Durbar were forgiven, differences between Sikh and Dogra were forgotten, and all Hindus, Muslims and Sikhs joined hands to defend their homeland. When it was learnt that the *Tunda lat* (Lord Hardinge) was himself coming up to the frontier to help Lord Gough direct the operations there was great excitement at Lahore. It is signnificant that in this time of national emergency, the Punjabis did not go to pray at mosques, temples or gurdwaras, but at the shrine of one who symbolised their sense of nationhood: it was the mausoleum of Ranjit Singh that became a place of pilgrimage. At all hours of the day and night, the garden round the mausoleum was crowded with people eager to get the latest news of the advance of the British armies towards their frontiers and hear the decisions of the *Panches* on how the country was to be defended.

The *Panches* went to the palace to get Rani Jindan's approval of their plans and to decide which of the officers would lead the army. One stormy meeting lasting four hours took place on 17th November 1844. There were some like Bhaia Ram Singh and Fakir Azizuddin who did not believe that the British would cross the Sutlej and that their preparations were as defensive as those of the Punjabis. This argument did not convince anyone. If the British measures were purely defensive, they asked, what was the pontoon bridge over the Sutlej meant for? Why had Ferozepur, which was only forty miles from Lahore, been militarized? And didn't the provision depot being set up at Bassian near the Sutlej, indicate that the British intended to have it behind them when their troops were fighting in the Punjab? And why in the last five years when the Punjabis were helping them in Afghanistan had the British more than trebled their army and guns, mustered the largest force ever known on the plains of India, on the Punjab frontier? There was no answer to this last argument. When Lord Ellenborough had left India the British force on the Punjab frontier (exclusive of hill-station garrisons) was 17,612 men and sixty-six guns. In the autumn of 1845 this had become 40,523 men and ninety-four guns. Till 1809, the only British military outpost was at Ludhiana. Now Ambala and Ferozepur had been fortified: cantonments had been built in the hills not far from the Sutlej at Sabathu, Kasauli and Dagshai. Large reserves were posted at Meerut and Delhi. It was quite clear to the Punjabis that the British had been preparing to invade their country for some years and since it was the right time of the year for English soldiers to fight in the plains, the army massed on the frontier was poised for an invasion and only awaited the Governor-General and the Commander-in-Chief to cross the pontoon bridge and take the road to Lahore.

The consensus of the meeting of 17th November was that the British were bent on war with the Punjabis and that their aggression was to be resisted at all cost. The

Durbar army was split up into seven divisions: four were ordered to proceed against British advance points at Rupar, Ludhiana, Harike and Ferozepur; two were to man the other frontiers, one, the Southern alongside Sindh, the other, the North-Western at Peshawar and Attock; one was to remain at Lahore. Each division was to consist of between 8,000 and 12,000 men.

The British Agent asked for an explanation of the military preparations. The Punjab Government replied that they were a counter-measure to their own preparations. In addition, the Durbar repeated its demand for the return of the treasure of Suchet Singh Dogra held by the British and the restoration of the village of Moran in Nabha to the Durbar's nominee, Dhanna Singh. The village in question had been given to Ranjit Singh by the Raja of Nabha in 1819 in exchange for land in the Punjab. Ranjit Singh had given the village to Dhanna Singh Malwai. The Raja of Nabha forcibly occupied and looted Moran in 1843. Despite the protest of the Durbar, the British had upheld the action of the Nabha Raja). Finally, there was the question of a free passage to the Punjab armed constabulary to Durbar possessions across the Sutlej—a right that had been acknowledged by the British on paper but more often than not denied in practice.

The British Agent was not satisfied with these answers and on 3rd December 1845 handed the Durbar's representative his passport. This severed diplomatic relations with Durbar. For all practical purposes the two States were at war.

The call to arms had gone out earlier. The latest manifestation of hostile intention created an atmosphere of feverish haste. Peasants and Chiefs left their homes and occupations to join the colours. The bard Shah Mohammad says:

> Sons of Sardars–handsome, dashing, debonair–
> Leapt to battle as lions leap out of their lair.

On 8th December 1845, British units from Meerut and Ambala under the command of Lord Gough, the Commander-in-Chief, moved northwards to join forces with General Littler's army at Ferozepur. The Punjabi Generals realised that if the two enemy armies were allowed to join forces, they would certainly be able to cross the river over the pontoon bridge and march straight towards Lahore. The Durbar army was given marching orders. The plan was to keep General Littler where he was and to intercept the column advancing under Gough and Hardinge.

It is still uncertain as to when exactly the Durbar army crossed the Sutlej. According to some Indian historians, it started to cross over in boats on 14th December; and since the entire flotilla consisted of 24 small boats, the operation was not completed till the 16th. According to British records, the crossing began on 11th December over the ford at Hari Ka Pattan. The news of the crossing was received by Lord Hardinge two days later and he declared war against the Durbar. Some Indian historians further maintain that Durbar troops crossed over into territory which had been recognised by the Treaty of 1809 as being he Durbar's property and therefore did not commit aggression. The British Government maintained that the crossing was a violation of the Treaty of 1809 and amounted to an act of war.

Lord Hardinge made the proclamation of war from his camp at Lashkari Khan ki Sarai. He recapitulated the friendly relations that had existed between the British and Ranjit Singh since the Treaty of 1809, the provisions of which, according to Hardinge, had been faithfully observed by the British but grossly violated by the Durbar in recent months. He claimed that British military movements were 'precautionary measures for the protection of the British frontier' and continued: 'The Sikh army has now, without a shadow of provocation, invaded the British territories.' The Governor-General declared the confiscation of the territories of the Durbar on the left bank of the Subje and called upon the Chiefs and Sardars in the protected territories to cooperate with the British in punishing the common enemy.

Despite the forthright language of the proclamation of war, Lord Hardinge was full of doubts. Five days later he remarked to Robert Cust, Personal Assistant to Broadfoot: 'Will the people of England consider this as an actual invasion of our frontier and a justification of war?' It is not surprising that Cust referred to the advance of the British forces as 'the first British invasion of the independent Kingdom of the Punjab'.

The opinions of two other British officers closely connected with Anglo-Punjab politics are worth noting. Major G. Carmichael Smyth of the North-western Agency, wrote: 'Regarding the Punjaub war; I am neither of the opinion that the Seiks made an unprovoked attack, nor that we have acted towards them with great forbearance . . . if the Seiks were to be considered entirely an independent state in no way answerable to us, we should not have provoked them!—for to assert that the bridge of boats brought from Bombay, was not a *causa belli*, but merely a defensive measure, is absurd; besides the Seiks had translations of Sir Charles Napier's speech (as it appeared in the Delhi Gazette) stating that we were going to war with them; and as all European powers would have done under such circumstances, the Seiks thought it as well to be first in the field. Moreover they were not encamped in our territory, but their own.

'. . . and I only ask, had we not departed from the rules of friendship first? The year before the war broke out, we kept the island between Ferozepore and the Punjaub, though it belonged to the Seiks, owing to the deep water being between us and the island.

'. . . But if on the other hand the Treaty of 1809 is said to have been binding between the two Governments, then the simple question is, who first departed from the "rules of friendship"? I am decidedly of opinion that we did.'

Even more emphatic on the subject is Sir George Campbell, who was then posted at Kaithal (a Sikh state escheated by the British). He wrote: 'It is recorded in the annals of history, or what is called history, which will go down to posterity, that the Sikh army invaded British territory in pursuance of a determination to attack us. And most people will be very much surprised to hear that they did nothing of the kind. They made no attack on our outlying cantonments, nor set foot in our territory. What they did do was to cross the river and to entrench themselves in their own territory.'

The exact size of the Punjab army sent against the British is not known; but it is conjectured that it was of the same strength as the enemy with slight superiority in artillery. It mainly comprised Sikhs and Mussulmans. The artillery had always been manned by Muslims. The bard Shah Mohammad names Sultan Mohammad (son of Ranjit Singh's famous artillery-man, Mian Ghausa), Imam Shah and Elahi Bakhsh. The Punjab army also had small numbers of Poorabias and Gurkhas. Gulab Singh forbade the Dogras to join.

The Punjabis started with the handicap of being led by traitors. There is enough evidence to prove that at different times both the Chief Minister, Raja Lal Singh, the Commander-in-Chief, Tej Singh, and at a later stage, Gulab Singh Dogra, were in communication with enemy agents. There is nothing concrete to implicate Rani Jindan apart from her liaison with the traitor Lal Singh and his letter to the British 'to consider him and the Bibi Saheba as their friends'. Nevertheless the feeling among many people was that the Durbar and Jindan were primarily responsible for egging the soldiers into hostilities and then letting them down—the object being to teach them a lesson for having executed her brother, Jawahar Singh. The bard Shah Mohammad states in no uncertain terms that Jindan 'tore up the State from the floor'.

The first thing Lal Singh did on marching with his army across the Sutlej was to write to Capt. Nicholson at Ferozepur: 'I have crossed with the Sikh army. You know my friendship to the British. Tell me what to do.'

Nicholson replied: 'Do not attack Ferozepur. Halt as many days as you can, and then march towards the Governor-General.'

Lal Singh carried out Nicholson's behest. He detached Tej Singh with a force to march towards Ferozepur and took the rest of the army with him a few miles upstream where he entrenched in horse-shoe formation near the village of Pheru Shahr—(now described as Ferozeshahr)—with the river Sutlej behind him and seven wells with good drinking water in their midst. Then, as Nicholson had instructed, he detached yet another force and marched it off to meet the main British army advancing under Lord Gough and the Governor-General.

Battle of Mudki—18th December 1845

The force Lal Singh took with him was considerably smaller than the one the British were bringing up. Accordding to Capt. Nicholson, it was no more than 3,500 men. Capt. Cunningham estimates it to have been about 12,000 men with twenty-two guns. Whatever their own strength, the Punjabis were unpleasantly surprised at the large size of Gough's army and its advanced position. Apart perhaps from Lal Singh, no one was expecting to meet the enemy for another couple of days, when suddenly on the afternoon of 18th December 1845 they sighted the British encamped near the village of Mudki. Instead of retreating to more suitable terrain, Lal Singh ordered his men to fall into battle formation on absolutely flat ground with little or no cover for his guns except some sandy hillocks and brushwood. Punjabi snipers took their perches on branches of some tamarisk trees growing in the vicinity and before the enemy were within range, Lal Singh ordered his guns to open fire–thereby betraying their position as well as wasting valuable ammunition.

Lord Gough waited patiently till the Punjabi fire slackened. Then he got his guns in position with their beads drawn on the spots already revealed by flashes from the Punjabi guns and in a short but intense cannonade silenced them. Just before sunset the British Cavalry charged the Punjabi flanks. Lal Singh promptly deserted his men and retreated to the camp at Ferozeshahr. The men refused to give in. They fought a grim hand-to-hand battle against the more numerous enemy led by the most experienced commanders of Europe, Lord Gough and Lord Hardinge. The battle continued with unabated fury till midnight (and came thereafter to be known as 'Midnight Mudki'). Then the leaderless Punjabis, who had lost more than half of their comrades and fifteen of their guns, withdrew from the battlefield.

Mudki was a field action of not very great military significance. To the British even this skirmish was an unpleasant surprise. Their casualties were 872 dead and wounded. Amongst those killed were Quartermaster-General Sir Robert Sale, Sir John McGaskill and Brig. Bulton. Punjabi snipers had taken a heavy toll of British lives. The British realised that they were up against the most determined fighters they had met on the Indian subcontinent. Gough sent word to Ferozepur warning Littler not to be drawn into an action on his own but to join him as soon as possible. More reinforcements were ordered from Ambala, Meerut and Delhi. Lord Hardinge relinquished his superior position of Governor-General and agreed to become second-in-command to the Commander-in-Chief.

Battle of Ferozeshahr–21st December 1845

Lal Singh was safely ensconced behind the stockades at Ferozeshahr while his men were grimly fighting at Mudki. On paper the plan still was for Tej Singh to take Ferozepur from Littler and then join Lal Singh to fight the enemy coming up from Mudki. Far from accounting for Littler's force of under 8,000 men, Tej Singh, who had as many as 30,000 men under his command, did not even bother to keep a watch on enemy movements and allowed Littler to slip out of Ferozepur in broad daylight.

Gough and Hardinge had left Mudki at 2 a.m. on the same night and arrived at Ferozeshahr by 10 a.m., where Littler joined them in the afternoon.

Gough did not want to take the chance of Tej Singh coming down from Ferozepur to join Lal Singh at Ferozeshahr and immediately ordered an assault on the Punjabi entrenchments. The battle commenced at 4 p.m. on 21st December (which was the shortest day of the year), with a charge by Littler's Cavalry and Infantry. The Punjabis repulsed Littler's Hindustanis with terrible slaughter. Punjabi guns were well placed and fired with greater rapidity than the British. Gough threw in his cavalry. Punjabi infantry met the enemy charge with musket-fire and then in a hand-to-hand combat. When the light began to fail, Gough poured in all he had in one desperate advance of cavalry, infantry and artillery on all sides of the horse-shoe in which the Punjabis were entrenched. The battle raged with extreme intensity through the dust and gloom of twilight. A shell hit the Punjabi powder magazine which blew up with a tremendous explosion and set many of the neighbouring tents on fire. The Punjabis turned the misfortune to their advantage by falling on parties of the enemy who had penetrated their entrenchments. At midnight the moon rose over the Sutlej and lit up the battlefield giving the Punjabis yet another opportunity to liquidate enemy pockets. There was no fight left in the British, their men were parched with thirst for all the wells were in the Punjabi camp,—and it had turned bitterly cold. By 3 a.m.

(22nd December) the last of the enemy advance units of Sir Harry Smith's brigade were repulsed and every inch of the ground that had been lost earlier had been recovered.

On the night of the 21st and 22nd, the fortunes of battle were definitely on the side of the Punjabis. The British suffered terrible casualities; every single member of the Governor-General's staff had been killed or wounded: amongst the dead was the notorious Broadfoot. Gough had his horse shot under him. That frosty night, 'the fate of India trembled in the balance.' Sir Hope Grant, one of the British Generals who fought the Anglo-Sikh wars, wrote: 'Truly that night was one of gloom and never perhaps in our annals of Indian warfare, has a British army on so large a scale been nearer to defeat which could have involved annihilation. The Sikhs had practically recovered the whole of their entrenched camp: our exhausted and decimated divisions bivouacked without mutual cohesion over a wide area . . .'

Lord Hardinge sent his son and the Bavarian Prince Waldemar, who was his guest, back to Mudki with the sword he had been given for his services in the Napoleonic campaigns with instructions that in the event of a defeat all his private papers were to be destroyed. An entry in Robert Cust's diary shows that the British Generals had decided to lay down their arms: 'December 22nd News came from the Governor-General that our attack of yesterday had failed, that affairs were desperate, that all state papers were to be destroyed, and that if the morning attack failed, all would be over: this was kept secret by

Mr. Currie and we were concerting measures to make an unconditional surrender to save the wounded, the part of the news that grieved me the most.'

The British Commander-in-Chief, Lord Gough, admitted 'that some brave men lost nerve and urged retreat upon Ferozepur' but he had resolved, as he said in his own words, 'rather to have my bones to bleach honourably at Ferozeshahr than that they should rot dishonourably at Ferozepur'.

When at long last the sun came up on the plains of Ferozeshahr the worst fears of the British were confirmed. Tej Singh arrived with his army from Ferozepur, fresh and eager for battle. The British guns had little ammunition left to fire and their men were too exhausted to fight. 'We had not a shot with our guns, and our cavalry horses were thoroughly done up,' wrote Lord Gough. The British resigned themselves to their fate and expected the Punjabis to give them the *coup de grace.* The situation in the British camp at that time is described by Sir Harry Smith in his autobiography: 'The ammunition for our guns was fully expended, and our troops were literally exhausted, and we could not attack what would have been an easy prey under other circumstanaces.

Tej Singh's guns opened fire. The British artillery did not answer. Then, without any reason, the Punjabi guns also became silent and a few minutes later, Tej Singh ordered the army to withdraw. The battle-eager soldiers were bewildered. A Nihang drew his sword, rushed up to Tej Singh and asked him to explain his order. Tej Singh joined the palms of his hands together and said with great humility that he was doing this in the interest of the Khalsa as he wished to attack the enemy in the rear. The soldiers were mollified and followed Tej Singh. It was then that the men who had fought so gallantly at Ferozeshahr the preceding night discovered that their commander Lal Singh had also decamped earlier. Argument and dissension broke out in the Punjabi camp.

It did not take Lord Gough long to appreciate that Lal Singh and Tej Singh had fulfilled their treacherous undertakings and he ordered his troops to make one more charge on Ferozeshahr. The defenders who had expected Tej Singh to relieve them were taken by surprise. They fled from their entrenchments, abandoning their guns, 80,000 lbs of gun-powder and all their stores.

Thus ended the battle of Ferozeshahr—a battle won by the Punjabi soldiers but lost by their traitorous commanders.

Soon after the debacle, Tej Singh visited the British camp and had an interview with Lord Hardinge. What passed between the two is not known: but from the subsequent treatment the British accorded to the traitor, it is not hard to guess.

Buddowal—21st January 1846

The British army followed up its victory at Ferozeshahr by moving up to the river Sutlej where Gough decided to wait for reinforcements before trying to push on to Lahore. Lal Singh and Tej Singh did not avail themselves of the opportunity of fighting a weakened enemy. Ferozeshahr had taken much of the fight out of the Khalsa army and it readily believed the story that the British had suffered so much that they would not try to cross the river.

The complacent mood lasted a few days. Then information was received that large enemy reinforcements with guns and munitions were moving northwards from Delhi and Ambala. It was also learnt that these reinforcements would first halt at Ludhiana and then go downstream along the Sutlej to Ferozepur.

A Sikh force of 8,000 men with seventy guns was posted at Phillaur to keep an eye on the enemy movements at Ludhiana. It was commanded by Ranjodh Singh Majithia who had with him Raja Ajit Singh of Ladwa–the only Malwai chief who had joined his compatriots. The two Sardars crossed the river and in rapid marches liberated the forts of Fatehgarh, Dharamkote, Gangarana and Buddowal (which had been in the territory of Ladwa but occupied by the enemy) and encamped at Baran Hata, seven miles from Ludhiana. The Sikhs stole into Ludhiana Cantonment and set many barracks on fire. The enemy depot at Bassian was also threatened.

Lord Gough ordered Sir Harry Smith to go to the relief of Ludhiana. Smith went upstream from Ferozepur keeping a few miles away from the left bank of the Sutlej. Ranjodh Singh Majithia marched his column alongside the enemy and continued harrying him whenever the opportunity presented itself. Smith tried to make a detour when he came to Buddowal. Ranjodh Singh did not let him by-pass the fort and attacked his rear with great vigour and captured Smith's baggage train and stores.

Sir Harry Smith paid tribute to Ranjodh Singh Majithia's tactics at Buddowal. 'It was the most scientific made during the war,' he wrote in his autobiography. 'And had he known how to profit by the position he had so judiciously occupied he would have obtained wonderful success. He should have attacked me with the vigour his French tutors would have displayed and destroyed me, for his force compared to mine was overwhelming; then turned about on the troops at Ludhiana, beaten them and sacked and burnt the city.'

This was also the opinion in the Punjab. The bard Shah Mohammad says that Ranjodh Singh had an open road to Delhi. Apparently, Majithia had no support and was unwilling to follow up his success. He was also in danger of being trapped between the enemy force on the Sutlej and their advancing reinforcements. He withdrew a few miles from Buddowal and dug himself in near the village of Aliwal on the banks of the Sutlej.

A few days later Sir Harry Smith received the reinforcements he was expecting and turned on Majithia and Ladwa at Alival.

Aliwal–28th January 1846

The battle was fought on the morning of Sunday, 28th January 1846. The Punjabis formed themselves into defensive triangles and as usual started their cannonade before the enemy was within range. The British let the

Punjabis exhaust their fire, discovered the exact location of their guns and then moved in to attack the weakest flank. At the crucial hour, the officers, including the Commander, Ranjodh Singh Majithia, deserted their troops. The men refused to retreat and fought with desperate valour. When the British cavalry charged, Sikh infantrymen drew the enemy's lances towards their bodies to get close enough to smite the horsemen with their *kirpans.* 'Although their leader, Ranjodh Singh, was the first to fly and basely quit the field leaving his brave followers to conquer or lose, their courage never quailed,' wrote Humbley. 'Again they rallied and made one last and vigorous effort. Though defeat had made them desperate they fought like men who jeopardised all.' Large numbers were killed in battle; many were pushed into the river and drowned. Fifty-six Punjabi guns fell into the hands of the British.

Historians still dispute the importance of Aliwal. The official British version taken from Sir Harry Smith was that it was a great British victory. There are others who state that it was a mere skirmish magnified into a great battle by Smith to atone for his defeat at Buddowal. Dr. Andrew Adams in his *Wanderings of a Naturalist in India* writes: 'Aliwal was the battle of the despatch, for none of us knew we had fought a battle until the particulars appeared in a document, which did more justice to everyone concerned. As an Irishman would say, we gained a disadvantage at Budiwal, by the baggage of the army falling into the hands of the enemy; that no exaggeration could turn Aliwal into a victory; but shortly afterwards, a few shots, and the charge of a squadron or two in pursuit of a host of retreating Sikhs, were magnified into a grand combat, and thus the plain of Aliwal has been recorded as the scene of one of India's marathons.'

Sabraon–10th February 1846

Aliwal may not have been as great a victory as was later made out by Sir Harry Smith, but it did take a heavy toll of Punjabi armament and the initiative passed out of their hands to the enemy. The British Commanders could now bide their time till they had sufficient force to strike whenever they wanted to and at the most vulnerable point.

Which city would the British attack first, Lahore or Amritsar? That was the question uppermost in the minds of the Punjabi military commanders. Once again they made a foolish decision to defend both at the same time and divided their forces. The larger portion of the army was entrenched in a horse-shoe curve of the Sutlej near the village of Sabraon, so as to block the enemy advance to Lahore. Lal Singh was posted a little higher up the river at Harike to prevent a surprise move on Amritsar.

Punjabi entrenchments at Sabraon were on the left bank of the river with a pontoon bridge connecting them with their base camp. Tej Singh had a brick tower built from which he could watch the action; the tower was well behind the front line and close enough to the bridge for a quick getaway. The bridge was also guarded by Tej Singh's personal bodyguard. All this could be ascribed to personal cowardice, but the way Tej Singh dispersed his force leaves no room for doubt that he wanted to ensure the defeat of the Khalsa army. Big guns were placed behind high embankments and consequently immobilised for offensive action. The infantry was also entrenched and could not therefore be deployed to harass the invaders. The enemy was thus given complete freedom to move about and choose his time and point of attack. The greatest blunder that Tej Singh made was not to have learnt a lesson from Ranjodh Singh Majithia's defeat at Aliwal, namely that a river in the rear can be a death-trap. Or, perhaps, he knew the lesson too well! What little chance the Sikhs had of holding out against an enemy superior in men, munitions and leadership, was lost by treachery. In the first week of February, Lal Singh sent his emissary to the British camp with a map giving the disposition of the Sikh entrenchment at Sabraon. The British Commander was not one to rely on the word of a traitor and sent a young peasant lad into the Punjabi camp. The 'Sabraon boy', as he came to be known, confirmed the information sent by Lal Singh.

The Punjabi army had traitors to lead it at the front and traitors in the rear to stab it in the back. Rani Jindan sent for Gulab Singh Dogra from Jammu and entrusted him with the task of negotiating with the British. Punjabi Mussulman regiments, which had been left behind to guard the capital, were ordered to proceed to the Sutlej, and Dogras occupied the fort and the barracks in the Cantonment. Gulab Singh refused to forward provisions of gun-powder to the army at Sabraon and opened communications with the Governor-General, Lord Hardinge.

A delegation of Army *Panches* came from the front-line to make a representation to the Durbar. They complained loudly that their men had had nothing to eat for several days and had subsisted on parched gram and carrots pulled out from the fields. Rani Jindan told them that she had been given to understand that Gulab Singh had forwarded plenty of food and munitions. 'No,' protested the *Panches,* 'we haven't had rations enough for a bird to peck at—*chirian di hazri*—give us food, give us powder and shot or we will not fight.'

There was a moment of tense silence. Then from behind the screen where Jindan sat, a hand shot out and flung a bodice at the *Panches.* 'Wear that, you cowards,' shouted the Maharani. 'I'll go in trousers and fight myself.'

The men felt ashamed of themselves. 'We will go,' they shouted back, 'we will lay down our lives for your son and the Khalsa Panth.'

Punjabi inactivity after Aliwal allowed the British plenty of time to get fresh reinforcements, ammunition and a siege train. When all was ready they decided to leave Tej Singh where he was at Sabraon and to cross the Sutlej lower down at Ganda Singh Wala. This plan was abandoned as the peasantry in the neighbourhood was found to be extremely hostile. Instead, Gough and Hardinge decided to make a frontal assault on the Punjabi entrenchments at Sabraon and destroy their army at one blow. This was undoubtedly planned in the confidence that the Sikh commander was on their side.

On 7th February it began to rain heavily. For the next two days the sky remained overcast and the downpour continued unabated. The Sutlej began to rise and within forty-eight hours rose more than seven inches, making all the fords unfordable; only one rickety pontoon bridge connected the army entrenched on the left bank with its base. Lord Gough was quick to seize the opportunity. On the evening of 9th February 1846, he marched out of Ferozepur, and under cover of darkness, surrounded the Punjabis at Sabraon.

On the morning of 10th February 1846, a heavy mist spread from the river over the rain-sodden fields and enveloped both the Punjabi and British armies. When the sky cleared and the sun's rays dissipated the mist, the Punjabis found themselves encircled between two horse-shoes: facing them were the British who covered their entrenchments from one end to the other and behind them was the Sutlej, now in spate. This time the British artillery took the initiative. Sikh guns were quick to reply. Then both artilleries ceased fire. There was half-an-hour of nerve-wracking silence—and the guns began barking again. British cavalry made a feint charge and withdrew after confirming the exact location of the Punjabi guns. The cannonade was resumed by the British with better results. In two hours the British guns put the Durbar's artillery out of action. The Punjabis had in any case run out of powder and shell. British cavalry charged the Punjabi entrenchments from three sides.

The traitor Tej Singh was the first to fly. 'He ran like a *lunda kutta*–a dog with a docked tail,' said a soldier contemptuously. It appeared subsequently that Tej Singh had not only intended to desert himself but had even tried to induce other Sardars to do likewise. When Sham Singh Attariwala refused, Tej Singh taunted him; 'If you are all that brave, let's see you take an oath on the Granth. I know you will join me in the end.'

'Never,' replied the Attariwala Sardar, and swore that he would rather be killed than give way to the English. He dressed himself in pure white and went into the thick of battle.

Tej Singh crossed the pontoon bridge to safety. As soon as he was across, he had the bridge destroyed.

Before leading his men to what he knew would be his last battle, Sardar Sham Singh dismissed his syce and told him to return to his village, Attari; 'Tell them that Sham Singh will not be coming home.' The band which rallied around him were killed to a man.

'It is due to the Sikhs to say that they fought bravely,' wrote General Sir Joseph Thackwell, who was present at the battle, 'for though defeated and broken they never ran, but fought with their *talwars* to the last and I witnessed several acts of great bravery in some of their Sirdars and men.'

With Sham Singh Attariwala fell the bravest of the Sikh Generals, Gulab Singh Gupta, Hira Singh Topee, Kishan Singh (son of Jemadar Khushal Singh) and their Muslim colleagues, Mubarak Ali and Shah Nawaz, son of Fateh Din of Kasur. Most of the others leapt into the swirling waters and were drowned. It is estimated that nearly 10,000 Punjabis were killed in the action at Sabraon. All their guns were either captured or lost in the river. It was a complete and crushing defeat.

Lord Hardinge who saw the action wrote: 'Few escaped; no one, it may be said, surrendered. The Sikhs met their fate with the resignation which distinguished their race.'

Lord Gough described Sabraon as the Waterloo of India. He paid tribute to the Punjabis: 'Policy precluded me from publicly recording my sentiments on the splendid gallantry of our fallen foe or to record acts of heroism displayed not only individually but almost collectively, by the Sikh Sardars and the army; and I declare were it not from a deep conviction that my country's good required the sacrifice I would have wept to have witnessed the fearful slaughter of so devoted a body of men.'

The bard Shah Mohammad immortalised the heroic stand of Sham Singh's men at Sabraon. 'They squeezed the blood out of the whites as one squeezes juice out of a lemon,' he wrote. 'If only Ranjit Singh were there he would have been proud to see how his Khalsa wielded their swords.'

Shah Mohammad explained the result of the campaign in the following words:

O Shah Mohammad, without Ranjit such was our plight
We won the battles but lost the fight.

The traitors too were immortalised in doggerel verse punning on their names:

Laloo di lalee gaee, Tejoo da gea tej
Ran vich pith dikhai key modha aie pher.

Laloo lost the blush of shame
Tejoo lost his lustre
By turning their backs in the field
They turned the tide and battle yield.

Chapter 8

The British Enter the Punjab

Remnants of the Punjabi army, defeated on the southern banks of the Sutlej, reassembled at the village of Raiban, east of Lahore, to lick their wounds. They had neither guns nor ammunition nor any fight left in them. The rest of the Durbar's forces were scattered in distant parts of the State.

The British did not give the Punjabis time to re-muster and two days after their victory at Sabraon, they crossed over the pontoon bridge at Ferozepur and occupied the fort of Kasur. Gulab Singh Dogra went out from Lahore to receive them; he was acceptable to the British because not only had he kept aloof from the Sutlej campaign, but had also prevented the Dogras from fighting alongside the Punjabis. On 3rd February 1846, he had been assured by Major Lawrence that his interests would be considered in any settlement imposed by the British on the Durbar. He had also been informed by Lord Hardinge that the British did not intend subverting the dynasty of Ranjit Singh. The best that the Dogra could hope for under the circumstances was to win British support to his claim to be Chief Minister of the Punjab in place of the now defeated and discredited Lal Singh. He was shrewd enough to go first to the Army *Panches* and get their assurance that any agreement he made with the British would not be repudiated by them. Armed with this guarantee, he took Fakir Nuruddin (Fakir Azizuddin having died a month earlier) and Dewan Dina Nath with him, and tendered the submission of the Durbar to the British.

Lord Hardinge wanted to annex the Punjab outright; but he realised that this could not be done in the spring of 1846. Although the Punjabis had been defeated on the Sutlej, they still had considerable forces in other parts of the State. Besides 25,000 men at Raiban, there were 8,000 more at Peshawar and an equal number in the south near Multan. Hardinge's own force was 20,000 men of which only a small proportion were Europeans; and the Hindustani sepoys had shown up very poorly against the Punjabis. An all-out campaign would require more reinforcements which, in turn, would put a severer strain on the exhausted treasury. In any case the campaigning season was almost over and the English soldiers were most reluctant to fight in the intense heat of summer. For these reasons, Lord Hardinge decided to annex the Punjab in two stages, taking half each time. In the first stage he would take the Jullundur Doab, separate the hills (Kashmir and Hazara) from the plains and weaken the State by limiting the size of the Punjabi army, to facilitate the final take-over. In an official minute he wrote: 'A diminution of the strength of such a warlike nation on our weakest frontier seems to me to be imperatively required. I have, therefore, determined to take a strong and fertile district between the Sutlej and the Beas. This will cover Ludhiana and bring us within a few miles of Amritsar, with our back to the Hills. In a military sense, it will be very important—

it will weaken the Sikhs and punish them in the eyes of Asia. I shall demand one million and a half in money as compensation: and if I can arrange to make Gulab Singh and the Hill tribes independent, including Kashmir, I shall have weakened this warlike republic. Its army must be disbanded and reorganised. The numbers of the artillery must be limited. The Maharajah must himself present the keys of Gobindgarh and Lahore, where the terms must be dictated and signed.'

Lord Hardinge wanted the ruling clique to remain Sikh so that it could keep a balance of power with the Muslims, who formed the majority of the population. The British were at the time highly distrustful of Muslims. These were the terms which Hardinge instructed his Agent, Major Henry Lawrence, to impose on the Durbar.

On 15th February, Gulab Singh Dogra, Fakir Nuruddin and Dina Nath, along with Sultan Mohammed Barakzai and other Sardars, waited on Lord Gough at Kasur. The Commander-in-Chief refused to accept *nazars* from them as they represented a nation still hostile to the British. He soundly warned them of the fate that awaited them. 'Retributive justice required that the proceedings of the British Government should be of a character which would mark to the whole world that insult could not be offered to the British Government, and our provinces invaded by a hostile army, without signal punishment.' Gough had also received instructions to show special favour to Gulab Singh. He praised the Dogra in front of the Sardars for 'the wisdom, prudence and good feeling evinced by him in having kept himself separate from these unjustifiable hostilities of the Sikhs'.

The representatives of the Lahore Durbar spent the whole night discussing the terms of the treaty with Frederick Currie, Chief Secretary of the British Government, and Major Henry Lawrence, and in the end conceded all that the victorious British required of them. They agreed to relinquish 'in full sovereignty of the territory, hill and plain, lying between the Sutlej and the Beas' (the Jullundur Doab at the time yielded a revenue of £4,00,000); to pay Rs 1½ crore as war indemnity (which the British knew the Durbar could not pay); and to surrender all guns that had faced the British, pay off the army and limit its strength to the number at the time of Ranjit Singh.

Three days later, Maharajah Dalip Singh was escorted by Gulab Singh Dogra and Bhaia Ram Singh to the British camp to make his submission to the Commander-in-Chief and the Governor-General at the village of Lulliani. The Dogra acted as Master of Ceremonies for the Durbar. 'Gulab Singh's oriental form of expression was rather fine,' wrote General Sir Hope Grant, who was present at the meeting. 'If,' said Gulab Singh, 'my son or dearest friend were taken ill, I should immediately send for the most eminent physician, and throw the sufferer into his hands, request his advice, and make the patient swallow the physic prescribed. I now place the Maharajah in the hands of the Governor-General as that skilful physician. I know everything he will do with regard to him will be for the best, and for his advantage.'

Lord Hardinge replied with a speech praising Ranjit Singh and expressed the hope that the relations between the two States would return to friendly normality. Presents were exchanged and British guns fired a salute to the Maharajah.

The Governor-General resumed his march to Lahore, with the vanquished Maharajah in his train. British troops were cantoned at Mian Mir just outside the capital. The Maharajah's guardians were nervous of the reaction of the populace and asked for a British force to guard the fort. The request was granted and British troops were posted round the palace and at the Hazuri Bagh entrance to the fort.

On 8th March 1846, the Treaty of Lahore, embodying the clauses of the partial annexation of the Punjab, was signed. General Sir Hope Grant gives a vivid description of the scene: 'The hall of the durbar was inlaid throughout with looking-glass; lustres and chandeliers were suspended from the ceilings; in front of the hall was an open court with lofty arches, beneath which a fountain was playing, and in the adjacent wide extent of water lovely water-birds were disporting themselves–amongst them a beautiful scarlet flamingo luxuriated in the spray. Hanging silk drapery and shawls screened off the sun, and beautiful rich-coloured carpets were spread over the floor. Inside the hall were the young Maharajah, Dhuleep Singh, a pretty boy, and the Sikh chiefs, Raja Lal Singh, a fine jovial-looking fellow; Raja Tej Singh, one of the Generals, with a most disagreeable countenance, strongly marked with small-pox, and presenting a disgusting drunken aspect; Raja Runjodh Singh, who commanded at Aliwal, a handsome but an effeminate-looking fellow, and innumerable other chiefs. According to the custom of the country, handsome presents were offered, and amongst them the priceless and magnificent *Koh-i-noor* diamond, which was handed about from person to person as though it were of little value. It was set as an armlet, and was merely fastened to the wearer with a bit of red silk. It was upwards of an inch in length, three-quarters of an inch in breadth, and thick, in proportion. Two smaller stones, each of immense value, were attached to either side of the jewel.'

The signatories for the Durbar were Lal Singh, Tej Singh, Bhaia Ram Singh and Dewan Dina Nath. Two clauses of the agreement drawn up at Kasur were amended. Since the Durbar was unable to pay more than 50 lakhs of the total war indemnity of Rs. 1½ crores, Hazara and Kashmir were taken away from the Punjab (as Hardinge had planned) and Kashmir sold to Gulab Singh Dogra for a million pound sterling.

The Dogras found it impossible to take Hazara from the Pathan tribes who had availed of the Punjabi preoccupation in the Sutlej campaign to free themselves and had captured all the forts in the region. The British came to their rescue by taking over Hazara and compensating Gulab Singh by giving him additional territory adjoining Jammu. After settling the frontier between Kashmir and the Punjab, Captain Abbott was put in charge of Hazara.

The figure of a million pound sterling was subsequently reduced by one-fourth. Suchet Singh's treasure estimated to be worth fifteen to twenty lakhs of rupees, which was with the British, was also given over to Gulab Singh.

The Durbar army was reduced to 20,000 infantry and 12,000 cavalry.

At the request of Lal Singh and other Sardars, a British force was kept for the protection of the Maharajah till the end of the year at a payment of £22,000. A Council of Regency was set up to administer the State on behalf of the Maharajah till he came of age. Rani Jindan became Regent with Lal Singh as her Chief Adviser. Major Henry Lawrence was posted at Lahore as Agent of the Governor-General.

On 16th March 1846, another ceremony took place in Amritsar. This was to ratify the treaty with Gulab Singh and formally give him the title to Jammu and Kashmir. The Dogra, who had only hoped to be Chief Minister of a truncated Punjab, became instead the Maharajah of a state about the size of Italy. Thus the *ricch* (bear), as he was known amongst the people, got the best honey out of the Durbar's honeycomb. He accepted the gift with due humility, describing himself unwittingly as *Zar Kharid*—a slave bought by gold.

Chapter 9

The Punjab as a British Protectorate

One month after the British had installed themselves as protectors of the Punjab there took place an incident which has come to be known in history as the 'cow row'. It indicates the state of mind of the 'protectors' and their attitude towards the natives.

An English sentry, irritated by an obstruction caused by a herd of cows, slashed some of them with his sword, and thus outraged the religious susceptibilities of the Hindu and Sikh citizens. The British Agent and officers who went into the city to explain the misconduct of the sentry were pelted with stones. They demanded the severest punishment for the insult. The next day Maharajah Dalip Singh was taken by Lal Singh to make his apologies to the Agent. Many houses in the bazar where the incident had taken place were razed to the ground and of the three men chiefly concerned in the stoning one was hanged and two deported. The English soldier who had caused the riot was 'warned to be more careful in the future'.

Not all Punjabis accepted the terms of the Treaty of Lahore and at least two expressed defiance in no uncertain terms. The commander of the fort of Kangra refused to obey the order of the Durbar to hand over the citadel to the British; he replied haughtily that he would not open the gates 'until Maharajah Ranjit Singh ordered him to do so' and obey no *purwana* save that of the powder and ball *(goley barood da purwana)*. In May, Henry Lawrence proceeded to Kangra with a combined British and Punjabi force to compel the fort to surrender–which it did on 28th May 1846.

A somewhat different situation obtained in Kashmir. The Governor, Shaikh Imamuddin, was informed of the treaty by which the State had been sold to Gulab Singh. He had hoped to keep it for himself. Later he received a secret message from Lal Singh, who had been chagrined by Gulab Singh's success with the English, that if he kept out the Dogras, Kashmir would be given to him, One of the messages read:

'My friend, you are not ignorant of the ingratitude and want of faith which Raja Gulab Singh has exhibited towards the Lahore Sarkar. It is indeed sufficiently glaring. I now write, therefore, to request you, my friend, that you will now set before your eyes the example of your late father's former relations with the aforesaid Raja, and consider both your duty and your interest to lie this way, and inflict such injury and chastisement upon the said Raja that he shall have reason to remember it. It is to be hoped he will never be able to re-establish himself again. For your security and confidence, my friend, I have sent you a separate written guarantee, that you may have no misgivings as to the consequences. Let me hear often of your welfare.

'P.S. Tear up this paper when you have read it.' Imamuddin had no difficulty in expelling the Dogras who came to take possession of Kashmir.

Gulab Singh appealed to the British Agent, who, in his turn, required the Durbar to fulfil its obligations under the Treaty.

In October 1846, Henry Lawrence took 17,000 Durbar troops along with Gulab Singh and his Dogras and proceeded to Kashmir. Shaikh Imamuddin submitted without firing a shot. In addition to handing over Kashmir, he handed over three secret missives he had received from Lal Singh exhorting him to resist Gulab Singh.

Lal Singh was tried by a British court, found guilty of duplicity and sentenced to be exiled from the Punjab. Apart perhaps from Rani Jindan, no one wasted any tears over the traitor. Even Dewan Dina Nath, who defended him in Court, agreed that having been proved guilty he should be externed. Lal Singh lived in peaceful obscurity in Dehra Dun and Mussoorie till his death in 1867.

The Council of Regency was reorganised with four members: Tej Singh, Dina Nath, Fakir Nuruddin and Sher Singh Attariwala.

While Lal Singh's trial was going on, Lehna Singh Majithia, who had returned from his rather lengthy 'pilgrimage' to Hindu holy places in India, called a meeting of some fifty leading Sardars of the State. They deliberated for some months to draw up a code of simple laws for the guidance of the Sikhs. But as the people began to get restive against their 'protectors' and in many places in the annexed Jullundur Doab there was rebellion against the administration of John Lawrence, the Majithia Sardar again quit the Punjab to resume his itinerary of homage to the Hindu gods.

In December 1846, Lord Hardinge again visited Lahore to review the working of the Treaty and to revise it in such a way as would facilitate the complete annexation of the Punjab.

Under the terms of the Treaty, the British force for the protection of the Maharajah had to be withdrawn by the end of the year. Hardinge did not want to withdraw this force; but he wanted to get the Durbar to ask for its retention. The Durbar was somewhat reluctant to make the request. In a letter dated 10 December 1846, Hardinge wrote to Currie: 'The coyness of the Durbar is natural; but it is very important the proposal should originate with them; and in any documents proceeding from them this admission must be stated in clear and unqualified terms; our reluctance to undertake a heavy responsibility must be set forth.'

In another letter, Lord Hardinge instructed Currie to 'persevere in your line of making the Sikh Durbar propose the condition or rather their readiness to assent to any conditions imposed as the price of the continuance of our support'.

'In the preamble of the Supplementary Articles', the Governor-General added, 'this solicitation must clearly be their act.'

Rani Jindan, who had been most anxious to have British troops in the capital, had had second thoughts after the fall of Lal Singh; she was eager to assert her own rights as the Queen Mother and get the foreigners out of the Kingdom. Hardinge decided to get rid of Jindan and make the British Resident *de facto* ruler of the Punjab. On 10th December 1846, he wrote to Frederick Currie: 'You are the person best qualified to ensure the success of a British administration under novel and difficult circumstances in the Punjab and in such case I should place you on the same footing as the Lieutenant-Governor . . . I have a very high opinion of Lawrence and next to yourself I prefer him.'

The British did not find it too difficult to get round the ministers. Their *jagirs* were confirmed, two leading Sardars, Sher Singh Attariwala, whose sister was engaged to the young Maharajah, and Tej Singh were handsomely rewarded–the former being made a *deodhidar* and the latter a Raja. A charade was enacted at Lahore. The English garrison packed up and made noisy preparations to leave; the ministers made an earnest appeal for it to stay; and the British Government reluctantly acceded to the request. The garrison returned to their barracks and unpacked their kit.

The Second Treaty of Lahore—16th December 1946

Lord Hardinge required the Treaty of Lahore of March 1846 to be amended to incorporate the changes. In so doing he desired that it be made clear that apart from paying for the upkeep of the British force (which the Durbar was doing already), the Durbar should agree that during the minority of Dalip Singh (till he was sixteen on 4th September 1854), the British Government undertook 'the maintenance of an administration, and the protection of the Maharajah Duleep Singh during the minority of His Highness.' The Resident was given full authority over all matters in every department of the State and the Governor-General was 'at liberty to occupy with British soldiers such positions as he may think fit, for the security of the capital, for the protection of the Maharajah, and the preservation of the peace of the country'.

It is important to bear in mind that by the Second Treaty of Lahore (which is also known as the Treaty of Bhairowal because Hardinge ratified it in his camp at Bhairowal), the Resident became the Governor of the Punjab and was quite independent of the Council of Regency of eight ministers. This was clearly stated by Lord Hardinge: 'It is politic that the Resident should carry the Native Council with him, the members of which are, however, entirely under his control and guidance; he can change them and appoint others, and in military affairs his power is unlimited as in the civil administration; he can withdraw Sikh garrisons, replacing them by British troops, in any and every part of the Punjab. In all our measures taken during the minority we must bear in mind that by the Treaty of Lahore, March 1846, the Punjab never was intended to be an independent State. By the clause I added, the Chief of the State can neither make war nor peace nor exchange nor sell an acre of territory, nor admit an European Officer, nor refuse us thoroughfare through his territories, nor, in fact, perform any act (except its own internal administration) without our permission. In fact, the native Prince is in fetters, and under our protection, and must do our bidding.'

The Treaty of Bhairowal also deprived Rani Jindan of all power; she was pensioned off with an annuity of Rs 1½ lakhs.

Even from the seclusion of the *zenana*, Jindan made her influence felt. Since all the adult male members of the royal family were dead and Dalip Singh was an infant, the protective instinct of the masses began to be projected on the widow. Jindan began to acquire a sort of heroic mysticity. She was the Queen Mother woefully wronged by the *ferinighi*. The Resident decided to get her out of his way.

The first attempt to get rid of Jindan was made in February 1847. A certain Prema was charged with the design to assassinate the British Resident and Tej Singh on the festival of Basant Panchmi. Prema was on visiting terms with a clerk of Jindan and it was suggested that the Maharani was an accessory to the plot. The evidence submitted was meagre and Hardinge advised the Resident not to pursue the matter against Jindan. He wrote: 'I do not consider that Her Highness ought to be held responsible for acts of interference of her confidential Secretary in communication with Prema, the chief conspirator in the plot to kill Tej Singh. The evidence is inconclusive, and I have rejected it.' Nevertheless, he encouraged the Resident to try other means of removing Jindan. He wrote: 'If we could get rid of her, it would give the little boy a better chance of being educated.'

The second move against Jindan was as clumsy as the first but the Resident secured the Governor-General's approval for it. He called a Durbar on 7th August 1847 and asked Dalip Singh to confer titles on fifteen Sardars who had rendered meritorious services to the British;

heading the list was the name of the traitor Tej Singh. When Tej Singh went up to the throne to receive the honour, the Maharajah joined the palms of his hands and refused to put the saffron mark on the Sardar's forehead. 'His Highness shrunk back into his velvet chair, with a determination foreign both to his age and gentle disposition,' wrote Henry Lawrence to his Government. The Resident saw the invisible hand of the Queen Mother behind the episode and two days later announced Jindan's banishment. In August, the Maharani was removed from Lahore because the Governor-General, who, in his own words, had 'the interests of a father in the education and guardianship of the young Prince, felt it had become absolutely necessary to separate the Maharajah from the Maharani, his mother'.

Jindan's allowance was reduced to less than one-third of the original (Rs. 48,000 per year) and she was put under house arrest in the fort of Sheikhupura. The Maharani echoed the sentiments of the people when she wrote to Henry Lawrence: 'Surely, royalty was never treated in the way you are treating us! Instead of being secretly King of the country, why don't you declare yourself so? You talk about friendship and then put us in prison. You establish traitors in Lahore, and then at their bidding you are going to kill the whole of the Punjab.'

Chapter 10

Bhai Maharaj Singh and the Banishment of Jindan

One year of the Resident's rule convinced the Punjabis that the British would take over the rest of the country as soon as they had consolidated their earlier conquest. A sense of resentment began to grow and soon focused itself round a peasant leader, Maharaj Singh of the village of Rabbon near Ludhiana. Maharaj Singh had been associated with Bhai Bir Singh and was present when the Bhai fell in the skirmish with the Durbar troops in 1844. Maharaj Singh succeeded to Bir Singh's vicarage at Naurangabad and soon became as influential with the Sikh peasantry and nobility of the Majha, Doaba and Malwa, as his predecessor. He came to be known as the Guru. Amongst the people who came under Maharaj Singh's religious and political influence was Rani Jindan and some of the Sardars of the court. The Bhai addressed large meetings of peasants in different parts of Central Punjab exhorting them to unite for the defence of their country. He rescued the name of Rani Jindan from the low level to which it had been reduced by bazar gossip and elevated it to the status of the Mother of the Khalsa. The British Resident was quick to sense that the Bhai's propaganda would jeopardise his Government's plans to annex the Punjab and issued warrants for his arrest. The Bhai eluded the police and wherever he appeared, large crowds gathered to hear him speak. The Resident felt that the next best he could do was to find some excuse for removing Rani Jindan who had become the symbol of Punjabi resurgence.

In May 1848, a conspiracy to tamper with the loyalty of native soldiers was unearthed. After a summary trial, three men were hanged and one sentenced to transportation for life. The Resident was of the opinion that Jindan was deeply implicated in the conspiracy and despite the admission that 'legal proof of the delinquency of the Maharani would not perhaps be obtainable,' and the knowledge that the entire Council of Regency was strongly opposed to his point of view, ordered her deportation from the Punjab. Jindan's baggage was subjected to a thorough search but nothing incriminating was found in it. The officers who carried out the order of search, arrest and deportation stripped the Maharani of 'several *pataras* containing jewels of great value'. She was taken to Benares under a heavy armed escort and her allowance was once again reduced to Rs. 12,000 a year.

The treatment accorded to Jindan outraged the sentiments of the people. They had almost forgotten her existence in Sheikhupura; her influence, wrote Edwardes, 'had followed her power, and there was no longer a man found in the Punjab who would shoulder a musket at her bidding.' That influence was suddenly revived by the Resident's action. A week after the deportation, the Resident wrote to the Governor-General that: 'The Khalsa soldiery on hearing of the removal of the Maharani was much disturbed: they said that she was Mother of the

Khalsa and that as she was gone and the young Dalip Singh is in our hands they had no longer anyone to fight for and uphold . . .'

Even Dost Mahommed, Amir of Afghanistan, expressed himself in sympathy with the people of the Punjab. In a letter to Captain Abbott, Dost Mahommed wrote: 'There can be no doubt that the Sikhs are daily becoming more and more discontented. Some have been dismissed from service, while others have been banished to Hindostan, in particular the mother of Maharajah Duleep Singh, who has been imprisoned and ill-treated. Such treatment is considered objectionable by all creeds, and both high and low prefer death.'

These statements were made in the context of an incident that occurred in Multan a month earlier and threatened to convulse the Punjab.

The district of Multan had been farmed by Dewan Sawan Mal Chopra, an extremely good administrator, until his murder in 1844. Sawan Mal left five sons, of whom the eldest, Mulraj, had administered Jhang and his younger brother, Karam Narain, had been in charge of Leiah. Of these three members of the family the only one who did not enjoy a high reputation was Mulraj. It was a common saying amongst the people that while Multan had been blessed with monsoon showers (*sawan*) and Leiah with *karam* (grace), Jhang had been afflicted with the corn weevil (*mula*). Mulraj was 'rich, in inferior health and without children, timid, unpopular with the army and people'. Nevertheless, Mulraj or Mula, as he was commonly known, was appointed to succeed his father and was ordered to pay Rs. 30 lakhs as succession fee. The turmoil at Lahore in the years 1844 and 1845 followed by the Sutlej wars and the British occupation of Lahore encouraged Mulraj to withold payment. When the Acting Resident took over the Durbar affairs, he accepted a representation of the Dewan and reduced the sum payable to Rs. 20 lakhs but at the same time took away the district of Jhang, north of the Ravi, which formed a third of Mulraj's estate. He also raised the revenue of what remained with Mulraj by more than a third for the next three years: he was asked to pay Rs. 19,68,000 for the territory for which his father had paid only Rs. 13,74,000. The Dewan accepted these conditions but soon found himself unable to raise the money because the excise duty on goods transported by river, which formed a substantial part of his income, was abolished by a fiat of the Resident. The Resident also assumed appellate powers on decisions made by Mulraj. The Resident was advised by Mulraj's enemy, Raja Lal Singh, who was further instigated by Karam Narain, who had fallen out with his brother and had taken up residence in Lahore. For these reasons, the Dewan put in his resignation in December 1847. He was persuaded to continue in his post till March 1848 by which time the winter harvest would be gathered in.

Mulraj's resignation gave the British an excellent opportunity to extend their hold on a large portion of independent Punjab. Appearances had however to be kept up. A Punjabi officer, Kahan Singh Man, was appointed to replace Mulraj. With the Sardar were sent two British officers, Vans Agnew of the Civil Service and Lt. Anderson of the European Fusiliers, who was an Oriental scholar, and having worked under Napier, knew Sindh and the Multan region well. The Englishmen were to be the real administrators of the Province. With the British officers and Kahan Singh Man was sent a force of fourteen hundred Durbar troops, a Gurkha regiment of infantry, seven hundred cavalry and one hundred artillerymen with six guns. The Englishmen went down by river; Kahan Singh marched with the troops.

Mulraj had resigned of his own free will. When his replacement arrived, he called on the officers to welcome them on their arrival at Multan and invited them to take over the fort. On 19th April the British officers inspected the fort and were formally presented with the keys of the gates. They installed companies of Gurkha infantry in the fort and dismissed the Multani garrison. Mulraj was escorting the visitors to the gate when a Multani, Amir Chand, infuriated by an order to salaam the Sahibs who had thrown him and thousands of his fellow soldiers out of employment, lunged at Vans Agnew with his spear and pierced his side. Vans Agnew lashed out at the man with his riding crop. Kahan Singh Man and Mulraj's brother-in-law, Ram Rang, rushed to Vans Agnew's assistance. In the scuffle that followed between the Multanis (both Hindu and Muslim) and the British party, Lt. Anderson and a few others were wounded. Mulraj rode back to the fort to his residence,

Amm Khas, to get help and sent a message to the British camp deploring the incident and promising to come over to see the injured men. Vans Agnew acknowledged Mulraj's letter exonerating the Dewan from complicity in the incident. He forwarded a report of the occurrence to the Resident at Lahore, stating clearly, 'I don't think Mulraj has anything to do with it. I was riding with him when we were attacked,' and sent an urgent message to Lt. Edwardes at Dera Fateh Khan and General Van Cortlandt, a Eurasian Officer in the Durbar's employ at Dera Ismail Khan, to come to his help. Meanwhile, Multani troops broke out in open revolt and forbade Mulraj from going to the British camp or handing over Multan to them. He tried to force his way through an angry crowd but was pushed back. Ram Rang, who was with him, tried to browbeat the mob. '*Namak haram,*' yelled the soldiers at Ram Rang. A scuffle ensued. A sepoy drew his sword and cut Ram Rang three times. Mulraj's horse reared and threw its master.

A pamphlet issued by the rebellious soldiers described the subsequent events in the following words:

'The soldiers then carried him (Mulraj) and Rung Ram off to their quarters, where they told them that it was the Guru's order to expel the *feringhees* by force. The Dewan would not consent that day. On the following morning, by God's will, the guns were fired, and the Guru ordered us to advance; for so it has been written in the Guru's writings. Upon this we obeyed his injunctions, and joining the Multanis, killed the *feringhees.*'

The Multanis swore to fight the British. The Pathans took their oath on the Koran, the Hindus on the Shastras and the Sikhs on the Granth. In the evening, they looted the British camp, carrying off all the provisions and pack animals—camels, bullocks and elephants. It is said, with what accuracy it is hard to tell, that the captured provisions included whisky, brandy, beer and hermetically sealed cans of meat and fish. A council was held to examine the goods. The whisky and brandy were retained; the beer rejected as *maila pani* (dirty water). After much deliberation it was opined by the wise counsellors that the lead tins could be nothing but shrapnel. Consequently next morning the guns of Multan fort opened fire on the Idgah and pelted the Durbar camp which had no food left, with shrimp, crab, fish and other delicacies.

The Durbar troops went over and joined the Multanis, leaving only Kahan Singh and a small escort of a dozen men and the Sahib's personal staff to defend the Sahibs.

On the evening of 20th April, the Multanis mobbed the Idgah. One Godar Singh, a Mazhabi Nihang Sikh, 'so deformed and crippled with old wounds that he looked more like an imp than a mortal man', came up to Vans Agnew, abused him and asked, 'Why have you come to Multan?' The Englishman did not reply, whereupon, the Nihang drew his *kirpan* and yelled: 'You become a Sikh or I will cut off your head.'

'I am a servant of Maharajah Dalip Singh,' pleaded Vans Agnew. 'Behold the hair on my head. What good will you do by killing me?'

Godar Singh roared, '*Boley So Nihal, Sat Sri Akal.*' He slashed Vans Agnew across the chest, caught the the Englishman by the hair and hacked off his head. A Pathan companion of the Nihang fired into the lifeless body. Somebody picked up Vans Agnew's head and threw it into Kahan Singh Man's lap with the taunt: 'Take the skull of the *launda*–lad–you brought down to govern Multan.' The Sardar burst into tears.

The mob then turned on Anderson and hacked him to bits. The rebels called on Mulraj and ordered him to become their leader. Mulraj consulted his mother. She told him that it did not behove a man to seek the counsel of women in such matters. She also reminded him that his father, the great Sawan Mal, had spent lakhs of rupees in strengthening the fort to be ready for an eventuality like one they were facing. This decided the 'chicken-hearted' Mulraj, who was notorious for his timidity, to become the leader of the rebellion. He rewarded Godar Singh with money and gave him Vans Agnew's bay horse and pistol. Godar Singh rode out in triumph. He rubbed powder into the dead man's hair and whiskers, thrust it in the mouth and nostrils and set fire to it. Thereafter the Multanis kicked the severed head about like a football, urinated and spat on it, shouting with glee, 'Look at the man who came to give us orders.' The city was illuminated at night. Godar Singh rode about brandishing his sword. When he met a clerk of the English party he shouted: 'Munshi, I will kill all your Europeans as far as Calcutta.'

The people of the neighbouring regions came to join Mulraj's colours. The Sikh troops issued an appeal to their co-religionists:

'Now we, in accordance with the Guru's command, have written to all of you, our Khalsa brethren. Those of you who are true and sincere Sikhs, will come to us here. You will receive pay, and will be received honourably in the Durbar of the Guru.

'The Maharajah Duleep will, by the Guru's grace, be firmly established in his kingdom; the cow and the Brahmin will be protected and our holy religion will prosper.

'All believing Sikhs, who trust in the Guru will place confidence in our words, and joining us, be received by the Guru and all his omissions and misdeeds will be pardoned by the Guru and his five *pyaras*.

'Forward copies of this manifesto to all our Sikh brethren, and delay not; for those who spread this intelligence will meet with the approbation of the Guru.

'You know that all are mortal; whoever therefore, as becomes a sincerely believing Sikh, devotes his life to the service of the Guru, will obtain fame and reputation in this world.

'The Maharajah and his mother are in sorrow and affliction. By engaging in their cause, you will obtain their favour and support. Khalsaji! gird up your loins under the protection of the Guru and Guru Gobind Singh will preserve your honour. Make much of a few words. Dated 12th Baisakh 1905 (22nd April 1848).'

Sikh soldiers appealed to the Sikh, Hindu to the Hindu, Mussulman to the Mussulman. In a few days, the Doabs between the Ravi and Chenab and the Chenab and Indus swarmed with Pathan and Baloch *shamsherees* (swordsmen). Mulraj found himself riding a tiger and knew that he could not now afford to dismount. Lt. Edwardes wrote to the Resident explaining Mulraj's predicament: 'I think Mulraj has been involved in rebellion against his will, and being a weak man, is now persuaded by his officers that there is no hope for him but in going all lengths; that the origin of the rebellion was the natural dislike of the Pathans, Baluchis and Multanies (men of high family, courage, and false pride) to be turned adrift, after a life spent in military service well rewarded; and that these men will fight desperately, and die hard . . .'

The immediate reaction of Resident Currie was to order troops he could spare towards Multan. But as soon as he got information that both Vans Agnew and Anderson were dead, he decided to bide his time and let the conflagration spread from Multan to the rest of the State, so that he could implicate the Maharajah, the Council of Regency, the Khalsa army and have the excuse to abolish all three. The order to the troops was countermanded and the Durbar coolly informed that since the revolt was against its authority it was for the Durbar to put it down, completely ignoring the fact that the British troops in the Punjab were being paid by the Durbar and it was their job to keep the Durbar in power by 'preserving the peace of the country'. The possibility of unrest had been foreseen by

Hardinge, who had organised three mobile brigades held in readiness at Lahore, Jullundur and Ferozepur to be able to take the field at short notice; these brigades were never called out. Currie also made a not too veiled threat that if the rebellion were not put down, the Council of Regency would be superseded. In a letter to the Governor-General, he wrote: 'The Chiefs returned yesterday morning, and having heard what I had to say regarding the necessity of their putting down the rebellion, and bringing the offenders to justice, by their own means as the only hope of saving their Government, they retired to consult and concert measures. After much discussion they declared themselves unable, without British aid, to coerce Diwan Mul Raj in Multan and bring the perpetrators of the outrage to justice. After what has happened, I feel that if the question were one merely affecting the maintenance of the Sikh Government and preserving the tranquillity of their province we should scarcely be justified in expending more British blood and British treasure in such service.'

The Resident was merely carrying out the policy laid down by the new Governor-General, the young and imperious Lord Dalhousie, who had a few months earlier replaced Lord Hardinge.

Hardinge had left, regretting that it had not been his fate 'to plant the British standard on the banks of the Indus'. Dalhousie had now grabbed the Union Jack and openly stated that he believed in 'grasping all rightful opportunities of acquiring territory or revenue as may from time to time present themselves'. Hardinge had assured his successor that 'it should not be necessary to fire a gun in India for some years to come'. Nevertheless, Dalhousie had proceeded to mass 50,000 men on the Sutlej, cantoned 9,000 in Lahore and 9,000 at Ferozepur. Four months after his taking over as Governor-General, the fracas at Multan–it was little more than that–gave him the opportunity he was waiting for. The question of rectitude did not unduly tax His Lordship's conscience.

Some British officers had the courage to speak their minds against this form of duplicity. Herbert Edwardes wrote a note to Resident Currie protesting that: 'Some of the hardest campaigns in Indian history were fought in the hot weather, and men do not sicken when their minds are on the stretch . . . There is an argument still stronger for our settling the affair ourselves. Our national faith as pledged in the treaty solemnly demands that we should do all in our power to preserve little Dalip's throne. Now if we wished to appropriate the country, and upset that throne, we have only to concentrate a Sikh army on Multan; and disloyalty would follow union, national insurrection would follow disloyalty, and the seizure of the Punjab in self-defence follow insurrection, as inevitably as the links of a chain. The world would acquit us, being ignorant of what we know; but neither God, nor our conscience could do so.'

The Durbar was on the horns of a dilemma, knowing full well that no matter what it did the result would be the same: the annexation of the Punjab. The only difference would be that if it did put down the Multan rising, the British would not have the excuse of subverting the dynasty of Ranjit Singh, and would probably only reduce Dalip Singh to the status of one of the Rajas of Hindustan. On the other hand, if it lent its support to the uprising this would lead to an all-out war against the British and a chance, however small, of winning and becoming free. Faced with these alternatives, the ministers did what anyone in their shoes would have done: to bide their time and see how the situation developed.

Maharajah Dalip Singh was still too young to be able to make up his own mind. His mother, the only one he could turn to for advice, had been removed from the scene. Her place had been taken by his prospective father-in-law, Chattar Singh of Attari, and his (Chattar Singh's) son Sher Singh. The old Sardar was Governor of the N.W.F. Districts. British officers were posted in close proximity to keep a watch on him; Major George Lawrence at Peshawar and his deputy, Captain James Abbott, at Hazara. Sher Singh assumed pre-eminence in Durbar circles by virtue of the fact that his sister was engaged to marry Dalip Singh. The Attariwala family were particularly cautious in their dealings with the British because they did not want to jeopardise the prospects of Dalip Singh becoming the sovereign (or even demisovereign) of the Punjab. They were determined to support the Resident in all measures he wished to take during the minority of the Maharajah.

The Resident instructed Sher Singh Attariwala and two other Durbar officers, Imamuddin and Jawahar Mal, to accompany General Whish on the expedition against Mulraj. The plan was to make a three-pronged attack on Multan: the Durbaris from the north, the Bahawalpuri Daudputras from the east, and the combined forces of General Van Cortlandt and Lt. Edwardes from the west or the south.

Up till then there was complete harmony between the Durbar and the Resident.

Suddenly the tone of Captain Abbott in his dealings with Chattar Singh Attariwala changed from polite to uppish and from uppish to insulting. It is hard to tell whether Abbott by nature was ill-bred and ill-tempered or was acting under instructions. He did however succeed in driving the old decrepit Sikh to desperation.

Let us return to Multan.

The populace had forced Mulraj to become their leader but he had barely 2,000 regular soldiers, five or six guns and a very limited quantity of gunpowder and ammunition with him. The rest of the Dewan's army was a mob armed with swords, spears and sharp-edged agricultural instruments. Coming against him from Lahore were European and Hindustani troops under General Whish and the Durbar's Punjabi battalions under Sher Singh Attariwala. On the north-western side he was threatened by Lt. Edwardes at Dera Fateh Khan with 2,000 men and four guns and Van Cortlandt with another 2,000 men a little higher up the Indus at Dera Ismail Khan. On his eastern side was the Nawab of Bahawalpur with his army. It was a desperate situation and Mulraj had no qualities of leadership. He was a frightened man, suspicious of the people who wanted to help him. Although he knew that the die had been cast he continued to protest his innocence with the Resident and asked for a fair trial. His family had accumulated a vast treasure, but he was reluctant to part with it.

The first move had been made by Lt. Edwardes. As soon as he had received the letter from Vans Agnew on 22nd April, he had crossed the Indus and occupied Leiah, but discreetly withdrew when he got information of a Multani force coming against him, and instead captured the small town of Mangrota from Mulraj's deputy, Chetan Mal. He exhorted the Muslim tribes of the neighbourhood to rise against the Sikhs. The prospect of loot induced many of the tribesmen to come in on the side of the British. Edwardes, Van Cortlandt and the tribal levies pushed southwards and on 20th May occupied Dera Ghazi Khan. Chetan Mal, who had retreated to Dera Ghazi Khan, was killed in a skirmish. Edwardes pressed on, by-passing the fort of Harrand, which was held jointly by Sikhs and Pathans, crossed the Indus and approached Multan from the south. From the other side troops from Bahawalpur (8,500 men, 11 guns and 302 *zamblooras),* commanded by Lt. Lake, crossed the Ravi to join Edwardes. Mulraj abandoned the post of Khangarh on the Chenab and proceeded from Shujabad to Kineri, where he clashed with the Bahawalpuris under Lake on 18th June 1848. Despite the

Bahawalpuris' superiority in men and guns, Mulraj held them at bay for seven hours till Van Cortlandt, who had occupied Khangarh, joined the Bahawalpuris. Mulraj fell back on Shujabad and from Shujabad on Sikandarabad and then on Surajkund, very close to Multan. The joint forces of Edwardes, Lake and Van Cortlandt, consisting of local tribesmen, Bahawalpuris and Durbar troops, inflicted yet another defeat on the Multanis on 1st July 1848 at Saddosam. The Multanis fell back on their citadel.

Meanwhile on the cool heights of Simla, Lord Gough was calmly planning a regulation campaign for the winter. 'As if the rebellion,' so runs an indignant letter from Edwardes, 'could be put off like a champagne tiffin with a three-cornered note to Mulraj, to name a date more agreeable.'

Mulraj's efforts to win over the Sikh soldiers to his side had not met with much success, because till then the Sikhs believed that Mulraj had rebelled against Maharajah Dalip Singh and the Durbar. But just about this time, Bhai Maharaj Singh arrived on the scene. He had toured the Majha country some time in May, exhorting the people to volunteer for the *Dharma yuddha*–the battle for righteousness. He told them of the prophecy contained in the *Sau Sakhi* (The Hundred Fables), a spurious piece of writing ascribed by charlatans to Guru Gobind Singh, wherein it was stated that in the year ensuing the British Government would come to an end and a man of the name of Dalip Singh would restore the sovereignty of the State and re-establish the Khalsa Panth. Thousands of Sikhs joined the crusade and made for Multan. The Resident ordered troops to pursue Maharaj Singh's private army. Durbar troops overtook Maharaj Singh near the Chenab. The Bhai was able to get away, but a large number of his followers were either captured or drowned in the river.

Bhai Maharaj Singh's arrival in Multan decided the rank and file of the Sikhs to throw in their lot with Mulraj. This is exactly what the British desired. They could now fan the spark of revolt and make it into a national conflagration, then drown it in blood and annex the state. The only obstacles were the Chiefs led by the Attariwala Sardars who remained doggedly loyal to the Resident. In June 1848, Sher Singh Attariwala was with the British officers investing Multan, while his father was policing the North-West Frontier. The Attariwala's adherence to the British exasperated the people. One Sujan Singh, who was the leader of a conspiracy to poison Sher Singh, was apprehended and blown off from a gun. 'Sujan Singh,' wrote Edwardes, 'was a Sikh *Jagirdar* horseman of some consideration and still greater notoriety.' This execution was extremely 'unpopular' and Sher Singh himself expected resistance.

The interests of the chiefs lay in the maintenance of the Resident's rule; the interests of the soldiers were against its continuance. The soldiers' *Panchayats* had been disbanded and their salaries reduced to the scale they had drawn in the time of Ranjit Singh. The Chiefs had had their privileges restored by the British and had much to lose; the soldiers had lost much; they had much to gain if the rebellion succeeded and little to lose if it failed. At the end of June, the Resident wrote that 'the Sirdars are true, I believe; the soldiers are false, I know.' Edwardes echoed the same opinion in the middle of July. 'With respect to the Sirdars, I believe them to be heart and soul on our side, which is the side of *jagirs,* titles, employments, and whole throats. But their force, with equal confidence, I report to be against us to a man.'

Anti-British sentiments gathered force as the siege of Multan dragged on. Chattar Singh Attariwala, who had earned a lot of unpopularity with the masses for his condemnation of the Multan rebellion (he had salutes fired in honour of Edwardes' victories over Mulraj), suddenly found himself let down by his English subordinate, Captain James Abbott. There were persistent remours that the British did not intend to honour their word about restoring the Punjab to Dalip Singh when he came of age. The old Sardar wrote to his son to get Lt. Edwardes to write to the Resident and fix a date for the marriage of Maharajah Dalip Singh to his (Chattar Singh Attariwala's) daughter. Edwardes approached the Resident, who promised to consult the Durbar. He ended his reply on an ominous note. 'I do not see how proceeding with the ceremonies of the Maharajah's nuptials can be considered as indicative of any line of policy which the Government may consider it right to pursue now or at any future time in respect to the administration of the Punjab.'

Captain James Abbot continued to behave aggressively towards Chattar Singh Attariwala. Early in August,

Chattar Singh was an old, bespectacled and bleary-eyed man who walked with a stoop and was in bad health. He was looking forward to getting his daughter married to the Maharajah and then retiring to his village, Attari. He did not want, nor was he fit enough to lead a rebellion. But the treatment he received at the hands of Abbott and Nicholson forced him to draw the sword with his feeble hands. He wrote to his son, telling him of the way he had been slighted by upstart foreigners and exhorted him to join his countrymen in fighting them to a finish. Till then Sher Singh Attariwala had stuck doggedly to his British allies and ignored the pleas of his soldiers and Mulraj's emissaries. On 9th September, he took part in an unsuccessful assault on Multan. Capt. Pearse recorded in his diary next day. 'The Sikhs fought splendidly—what pricks they are!' His father's letter made Sher Singh extremely uneasy. There were even rumours afloat that Chattar Singh had been murdered by Fateh Khan Gheba, a hireling of the British. But Sher Singh took no notice of them. An incident on 13th September 1848 finally convinced him of the dishonesty of British intentions. That night he visited the British officers' mess after dinner, as he had done every day, and took his seat next to Edwardes. He noticed Van Corlandt (still eating the Durbar's salt) slip out of the tent. A little later, an officer of Sher Singh's regiment came in and whispered in the Sardar's ear that Corlandt had ordered the mess tent to be surrounded by Pathan mercenaries. Sher Singh took a hurried leave and got away before Van Cortlandt's men could apprehend him. Next morning Sher Singh Attariwala and his troops left the British Camp.

Sher Singh issued a proclamation asking all Punjabis to rise against the foreign oppressors. It said: 'It is well known to all the inhabitants of the Punjab, to all the Sikhs, and those who have cherished the Khalsa, and in fact, the world at large, with what oppression, tyranny and violence the *feringhis* have treated the widow of the great Maharajah Ranjit Singh and what cruelty they have shown towards the people of the country.'

For three weeks Sher Singh Attariwala tried to convince Mulraj that he had broken with the *feringhi* but the Dewan refused to believe him. His suspicions had been further roused by a forged letter which Edwardes contrived to let fall into Mulraj's hands. In this letter Edwardes pretended to be privy to a plot by which Sher Singh was to take the fort by stratagem. The gates of Multan fort remained firmly shut against Attariwala. Sher Singh lost patience with Mulraj and on 9th October struck camp to go north to join his father.

The nation began to rise in arms.

The British were prepared for the contingency. On the north-west, Nicholson occupied the fort of Attock. Capt. Hodson (the same notorious Hodson who later executed the three Mughal Princes in Delhi) went to Amritsar, got admission into Gobindgarh fort on a false plea and then overpowered the guards. In Lahore, the Resident arrested all the people he suspected of having sympathies with the revolt, including Ranjodh Singh Majithia. In the

Jullundur Doab, John Lawrence put down anti-British demonstrations with an iron hand.

At Kohat, Chattar Singh opened negotiations with Dost Mohammed Khan, Amir of Afghanistan, and his brother Sultan Mohammad. He undertook to give them Peshawar if the Afghans helped the Punjabis to expel the English. To be able to make good his promise, he evicted the British officers, including the Resident's chief assistant George Lawrence, reoccupied Peshawar and wrested Attock from Nicholson. George Lawrence, who had taken asylum in Kohat, and Herbert, who had replaced Nicholson, were taken prisoners. The whole of Derajat was up in arms. Malik Fateh Khan Tiwana, who was the Resident's nominee, and the Eurasian turn-coat, Colonel Holmes, were shot by Sikh troops. Similar risings took place in other districts between Lahore and the Frontier. *The British Subaltern* wrote in his diary: 'Forces are daily joining the enemy: the whole of the Punjab is inimical to us and in case of the least reverse we should have them about our ears like a swarm out of an upset bee-hive.'

Thus did a local rebellion become a national war of independence.

There were two centres of revolt—one at Multan and the other on the North-West frontier. The British Commander-in-Chief, Lord Gough, suggested that the siege of Multan should be raised till reinforcements could come up from Bombay and priority be given to the campaign against the Attariwalas. Lord Dalhousie accepted the suggestion.

Dalhousie had made up his mind to declare war and annex the Punjab. He was pleased with the course of events. 'The insurrection in Hazara has made great headway . . . I should wish nothing better. I can see no escape from the necessity of annexing this infernal country. I have drawn the sword and this time thrown away the scabbard,' he wrote.

But who was Dalhousie going to war against? Maharajah Dalip Singh and the Council of Regency (except the Attariwalas) had not revolted. On the contrary, the rebellion of Mulraj, the Attariwalas and the soldiers was against the authority of the Durbar and its Sovereign-to be. If Dalhousie meant to suppress the rebellion, it was only logical and moral that he should uphold Dalip, the Council and the Durbar. But that was not Dalhousie's intention. He had fomented and nurtured the rebellion so that he could have the excuse of annexing the Punjab and no legal niceties were going to bother him. On hearing of the proclamation made by the Attariwalas, Dallhousie expressed pleasure because it had 'brought matters to the crisis I (Dalhousie) have for months been looking for and we are now not on the eve of but in the midst of war with the Sikh nation and kingdom of Punjab.' In a public pronouncement at a banquet on 9th October, Dalhousie said, 'unwarned by precedents, un-influenced by example, the Sikh nation has called for war and on my words, Sir, they shall have it with a vengeance.' Before leaving Calcutta for the Punjab frontier, Dalhousie instructed his Secretary to inform the Resident at Lahore that he considered 'the state of Lahore to be to all intents and purposes directly at war with the British Government'. The Resident persuaded the Governor-General that for reasons of expediency they should not declare war till all their troops were in position but keep up the pretence that the British had 'entered Lahore territories not as enemy to the constituted government but to restore order and obedience'.

Chapter 11

The Fall of the Punjab

Sher Singh Attariwala intended marching back to Lahore and liberating the capital. He came within two miles of the city, but the rising of the citizens which he had expected did not take place. The Resident had imposed a curfew and the streets were patrolled at all hours. The leading Sardars had been arrested. Lehna Singh Majithia had thrown in his lot with the enemy and was using all his influence in Majha, the homeland of the toughest of the Sikh peasantry, in favour of the British. The only chief who had the temerity to defy the British was Ram Singh of Nurpur; but his declaring for freedom was more symbolic than of material assistance to Sher Singh.

Sher Singh got information that Lord Gough was bringing a large army with heavy guns across the Sutlej. He withdrew from Lahore to join forces with his father. The Attariwalas decided to hold the British on the Chenab—'the dark river'.

The situation in the autumn of 1848 was somewhat as follows: The Chaj and the Sindh-Sagar Doabs had declared for freedom; the other Doabs were under the heel of British military power. In the north-west, people were flocking to the Punjab standard unfurled by Chattar Singh Attariwala; in the south, Mulraj was fighting a lone battle against odds that kept mounting against him day by day.

Early in November 1848, Lord Gough crossed the Sutlej with an army composed of English and Hindustani mercenaries and marched on to Lahore. Young Dalip Singh, who had done everything he had been told to do by the Resident, waited on the British Commander to pay his respects. Gough refused to receive thc Maharajah. On 16th November when the Resident himself took Dalip Singh to Mian Mir where the British force was cantoned, Gough did not get off his elephant to return Dalip's greetings. It was a deliberate act of discourtesy to signify that the British now looked upon the Maharajah (who still under their protection) as an enemy.

Gough advanced northwards to the Chenab and came in sight of the Attariwala's forces on the other side of the river. Sher Singh, who had captured some forts on the eastern bank, sent detachments to harass the British. Minor skirmishes between the Punjabis and the British took place along the left bank of the Chenab. In the last week of November 1848, British forces under Brigadier-General Campbell marched towards the fort of Ram Nagar. The Punjabis forestalled the move to capture the fort. They crossed the Chenab on 22nd November and placed themselves between the British and Ram Nagar.

General Campbell opened the attack and forced thn Punjabis back to the river. Punjabi artillery posted oe the opposite bank opened up. With the support of the artillery, more Punjabi cavalry crossed the Chenab and in a determined counter-attack routed Campbell's force, captured one of his guns and the colours of a regiment.

Ram Nagar was not an engagement of any great consequence but it gave a much needed booster to Punjabi morale. *The British Subaltern* wrote: 'The enemy are in great feather, and ride along within half a mile of our camp and close to our pickets.' Three senior British officers, Lt. Col. Havelock, Brig. Gen. Cureton and Captain Fitzgerald were killed at Ram Nagar. Sher Singh Attariwala sent a note to the British offering to stop hostilities if they promised to get out of Lahore. No notice was taken of this offer.

A week after the Punjabi victory at Ram Nagar, General Gough arrived on the Chenab but instead of assaulting the fort as the Punjabis expected him to do, went further upstream to Wazirabad, bribed the local boatmen and crossed the river under the cover of darkness. While Sher Singh Attariwala went up to hold Gough's advance down the western bank of the Chenab, the rest of the British force was able to cross the river over the fords which were left unguarded.

On the afternoon of 3rd December, an artillery duel was fought in the sugar-cane fields around the village of Sadullapur. The cannonade from either side was fierce. *The Subaltern* described the thunder as: 'A roar that shook the very earth and shot ran through the air with a noise like a mighty winged spirit till the atmosphere was stunned.' British superiority in guns gave them the edge over the Punjabis. Sadullapur was also not an engagement of any military consequence but was exaggerated by the British Commander as a great victory to offset the reverse suffered at Ram Nagar. They even had it noised about that

Sher Singh had been killed in the engagement. Attariwala was very much alive. He retreated from the Chenab to the Jhelum. The British pursued him across the Chaj Doab.

The Punjabis took up their position in the village of Rasul, which was surrounded by an expanse of thick brushwood intersected by deep ravines. The Jhelum was behind them. The enemy came up and took his position at the village of Dinghy about three miles southeast of the Punjabi entrenchments. For some time the two armies jockeyed for position. The Punjabis began to run short of provisions and tried to draw out the enemy from Dinghy. On 13th December, Sher Singh made a feint attack on the British positions but the British refused to budge. Next day came news of the liberation of Attock. Chattar Singh sent troops he could spare to his son and promised to join him with the rest of the army.

The British received even a greater fillip with the news of the fall of Multan. On 30th December, a British cannon-ball fell on the magazine in the fort blowing up 4,00,000 lbs of gunpowder and killing over five hundred of its defenders. The odds turned heavily against Mulraj particularly as the British received more reinforcements and siege-guns from Bombay. On 22nd January, Mulraj was compelled to lay down arms.

Victory at Chillianwala, 13th January 1849

Lord Gough decided to attack at once. His forces had been augmented by detachments of Dogras under Col.

Steinbach (one-time servant of Ranjit Singh) and Rohillas who had deserted the Punjabi camp. His plan was to avoid the jungles and ravines by going a few miles downstream and then attacking the Punjabi flank. Sher Singh forestalled this move and took up formation at the village of Lulliani–with the jungles and ravines still separating him and the enemy.

At noon on 13th January 1848, the Punjabis sighted the British advancing towards them from the direction of the village of Chillianwala. General Elahi Bakhsh's artillery brought the enemy advance to a standstill. For one hour Punjabi guns kept the British at a distance. When their fire slackened, the British, who had the advantage of numbers, charged in an attempt to force the Punjabis into the river. The assault was led by Brigadier Pennycuick. The Khalsa found the conditions to their liking. They scattered into the brushwood jungle and began their harrying *dhai-phut* (hit and run) tactics. Their snipers took heavy toll of British infantry and cavalry. Those that got through the brushwood and ravines were easily repulsed in the hand-to-hand fight with the main line of the Punjabi troops. Pennycuick, his son and hundreds of the enemy were killed in the most savage fighting between the Punjabis and the British. *The British Subaltern* wrote: 'The Sikhs fought like devils . . . fierce and untamed even in their dying struggle . . . Such a mass of men I never set eye on and as plucky as lions: they ran right on the bayonets of the 24th (Regiment) and struck at their assailants when they were transfixed.'

The bloody battle lasted till darkness fell. The Punjabis captured four British guns and the colours of three regiments. The night was one of great terror for the British. General Thackwell wrote: 'Confusion pervaded the whole army. Fears were generally entertained that the enemy (the Punjabis) would attempt a night attack. If they had been enterprising and could have perceived the extent of their advantage, they would assuredly have thrown themselves on us . . . the jungle which had befriended them in the commencement of the action now formed a protection to us.'

The scene of the next morning is also painted by General Thackwell: 'Prince Albert hats and military shoes might be seen in all directions strewn on the ground in great abundance . . . the camp next day was overspread with funereal gloom.' And it might well have been, for nearly 3,000 British lay dead or wounded in the ravines and brushwood.

Chillianwala was the worst defeat the British had suffered since their occupation of India. Gough was superseded and Napier was asked to come from England to take over command.

Sher Singh Attariwala's guns boomed a twenty-one gun salute to the Punjabi victory.

The British awaited their doom with stoic resignation. And once again, as at Ferozeshahr, the Punjabis failed to drive home their advantage to a conclusive victory. Their own losses had been considerable and they were not aware of the magnitude of the punishment they had inflicted on the enemy. They were short of powder and their artillery Commander, General Elahi Bakhsh, in a moment of weakness laid down arms. The supply situation became acute particularly as three days after the battle Chattar Singh with his troops joined his son with not enough provisions for themselves. The elements also came to the rescue of the British. As soon as the fighting stopped it began to rain; and for the next three days it poured incessantly, turning the ravines which separated the Punjabis from their quarry into deep moats. By the fourth day when the sun shone again on the sodden plain, the British had pulled out of Chillianwala and retreated across the Chaj to the banks of the Chenab.

The English poet, George Meredith, composed the following lines in commemoration of the battle.

Chillianwallah, Chillianwallah!
'Tis a village dark and low,
By the bloody Jhelum river
Bridged by the foreboding foe;

And across the wintry water
He is ready to retreat,
When the carnage and the slaughter
Shall have paid for his defeat.

Chillianwallah, Chillianwallah!
'Tis a wild and dreary plain.

Strewn with plots of thickest jungle,
Matted with the gory stain.
There the murder-mouthed artillery,
In the deadly ambuscade,
Wrought the thunder of its treachery
On the skeleton brigade.

Chillianwallah, Chillianwallah!
When the night set in with rain,
Came the savage plundering devils
To their work among the slain;
And the wounded and the dying
In cold blood did share the doom
Of their comrades round them lying,
Stiff in the dead skyless gloom.

Chillianwallah, Chillanwallah!
Thou wilt be a doleful chord,
And a mystic note of mourning
That will need no chiming word;
And that heart will leap with anguish
Who may understand thee best;
But the hopes of all will languish
Till thy memory is at rest.

Sher Singh Attariwala again sent a proposal for settlement. Since the Maharajah was in British hands, all he asked for was the reinstatement of Dalip Singh and the evacuation of British forces from Lahore. Sher Singh sent George Lawrence, who was a prisoner in his hands, as an envoy. The terms were rejected. More reinforcements were sent up from Hindustan.

One may be permitted to digress on the Punjabi treatment of British prisoners. It was always favourably commended by British soldiers—though not always by British historians. *The British Subalter* wrote: 'Two of the 9,000 lancers who were taken prisoners the other day were sent back this morning with Sher Singh's compliments. They seemed rather sorry to come back as they had been treated like princes, *pilawed* with champagne and brandy to the mast head and sent away with Rs. 10 each in his pocket.'

The Disaster at Gujerat, 21st February 1849

Sher Singh Attariwala advanced towards the Chenab and entrenched his forces in horse-shoe formation between the town of Gujerat and the river. At the ends of the horse-shoe were the dry beds of two streams. The British forces reassembled at the village of Lassori and then advanced on Gujerat: their right flank touching the Chenab, their left across the same dry stream-bed a little lower down. General Whish, who had been freed from the Multan campaign, came up and added to the enemy strength.

The Punjabis were weaker both in guns (fifty-nine to the British sixty-six) and in manpower. The Afghan Cavalry was led by Dost Mohammad's son, Akram Khan, but it could barely be relied on in a struggle which was essentially between the Punjabis and the British.

The engagement was fought on a bright, sunny morning, with larks singing in the sky. The British advance began at 7.30 a.m. The Punjabis were as usual lacking in confidence. They opened fire too soon and blew away ammunition of which they were short and betrayed the position of their guns. The British halted when they were within range, adjusted their sights and in a cannonade lasting an hour and a half silenced the Punjabi artillery. Then with their guns still belching fire, British cavalry and infantry stormed the Punjabis. The Afghan cavalry tried to deflect the enemy but withdrew without effecting their purpose and thus exposed another Punjabi flank to the enemy. The Punjabis received the British assault as they had done in the earlier engagements. 'In this action as well as at Chillianwala' wrote, Thackwell 'Seikhs caught hold of the bayonets of their assailants with their left hands and closing with their adversary dealt furious sword blows with their right . . . This circumstance alone will suffice to demonstrate the rare species of courage possessed by these men.' The gunners, both Mussalman and Sikh, literally stuck to their guns to the last. General Thackwell remarked: 'The fidelity displayed by the Seikh gunners is worthy of record: the devotion with which they remained at their posts, when the atmosphere around them was absolutely fired by the British guns, does not admit description.'

The Punjabis began to retreat. By noon they had evacuated Gujerat. The British occupied the town and pressed home their advantage by relentless pursuit. The Punjabis were hemmed in from all sides: Gough in front, Steinbach's Dogras on their right, Imamuddin on their left and Abbott's Pathan mercenaries behind them. The Commanders (except Sher Singh Attariwala, who had three horses shot under him) fled, leaving the common soldiers to fight a delaying rear-guard action. The men fought late into the night: their bodies were found scattered for many miles beyond the field of battle. The night was made more fearful by explosions of unfired Punjabi ammunition dumps and by the thunder and rain which followed. The enemy gave the Punjabi wounded no mercy. *The British Subaltern* wrote: 'Little quarter, I am ashamed to say, was given–and even those we managed to save from the vengeance of our men, I fear, were killed afterwards. But, after all, it is a war of extermination.'

The Battle of Gujerat was a disaster to Punjabi arms from which they could scarcely hope to recover. The *coup de grace* was however delivered by the arch-traitor Gulab Singh Dogra. He helped Abbott to cut off Sher Singh Attariwala's retreat towards the frontier. The prospect of continuing the fight with Afghan help was thus obviated. He also arranged for the supply of boats for the British army to cross the Jhelum. Sher Singh tried to negotiate terms but the British insisted on unconditional surrender.

On 14th March 1849, both the Attariwala Sardars, father and son, came to the British camp at Hurmel near Rawalpindi with their faces covered under their shawls and gave up their swords to General Gilbert. They were followed by batches of hundreds. 'The reluctance of some of the old Khalsa veterans to surrender their arms was evident. Some could not restrain their tears; while on the faces of others, rage and hatred were visibly depicted', wrote General Thackwell. The remark of one veteran greybeard, as he put down his gun, summed up the history of the Punjab: '*Aj Ranjit Singh mar gaya* (Today Ranjit Singh has died).'

Of 29th March 1849, Mr. Eliot, Lord Dalhousie's Secretary, called a *durbar* in the fort. Dalip Singh took his seat on the throne of the Punjab. Eliot then read the proclamation declaring the kingdom of the Punjab at an end. The *Koh-i-noor* diamond was handed over by the young Maharajah and he stepped down from his illustrious father's throne—never to sit on it again. Indeed, Maharajah Ranjit Singh was dead!

Postscript

What happened to the characters who played such dramatic roles in the downfall of the kingdom of the Punjab?

Maharajah Dalip Singh was only ten when his kingdom was annexed. In those ten years he had seen his mother grossly insulted by low upstarts, exploited by the ambitious, and misused by men of lust; he had seen relations and friends murdered before his eyes, and he had seen the best of men behave in the vilest manner. He was seated on the throne and had his feet kissed in public by men who had no compunction in calling him a bastard when they wanted to. He wore the world's greatest diamond on his arm but was denied expenses to maintain himself and his mother with dignity. He was a frightened, effeminate young man who had had enough of the Punjab and the Punjabis and wanted nothing better than to get away from both.

Lord Dalhousie appointed Dr. Login to be tutor-companion to Dalip and the two were allowed residence in Fatehgarh in Uttar Pradesh. Within a few months of the Englishman's tutelage Dalip Singh expressed the desire to renounce the Sikh faith, accept conversion to Christianity and go to England. Dalhousie was delighted to hear of this—not because he felt that the Church would gain an important adherent, but because it would forever kill Dalip's chances of being acknowledged by the Sikhs as their Maharajah. 'Politically we could desire nothing better, for it destroys his possible influence for ever,' he wrote. After two years of probation the young Maharajah's hair was shorn and he was baptized a Christian. Dalhousie was very moved by the event. 'If ever the finger of God wrote upon the wall, it did in the sight of this boy, and to the touching of his heart.'

Dalip also wanted to give up being a Punjabi and turn himself into an English country-gentleman. At first Dalhousie was a little apprehensive of this move, but then realised that he could turn Dalip's anglomania to the total destruction of the Sikh royal family. He decided that the Maharajah should be given a companion. The person chosen was Dalip's nephew, Prince Shiv Dev Singh, the son of the late Maharajah Sher Singh and the only other surviving member of the direct line of Ranjit Singh. The motive for the choice was candidly stated by Dalhousie. 'Shiv Dev Singh is an intelligent little boy with a foolish mother, who is too much inclined to puff up the child with notions that he is the only hopeful Maharajah now, since Dalip has become a Christian. Hence we thought it best for him to go with his uncle.'

Dalhousie presented Dalip with a copy of the Bible as a parting present 'as the best of all gifts, since in it alone will be found the secret of real happiness either in this world or in that which is to come'.

In England, Dalip Singh became a frequent visitor to Buckingham Palace and was treated by Queen Victoria as her godson. He was given an allowance of £40,000 a year and a large estate in the county of Suffolk. In

1861 he returned to India for a short while and took his mother back with him to England. Two years later he came back again carrying Jindan's ashes. On his way to India he met a half-caste girl, Bamba Muller, the daughter of an Abyssinian woman by a German trader, and married her in Alexandria. The two lived in Suffolk for some years and raised a numerous but undistinguished progeny.

Dalip and his Ethiopian Maharani became prominent figures in English social circles. They began to live beyond their allowance. The nagging of creditors and the hollow tedium of social life soon disillusioned the Maharajah with the European way of living. He began to toy with the idea of returning to India and reclaiming his kingdom. He opened correspondence with several Indian Princes and Sikh Sardars. To make his chances better, he renounced Christianity with the same alacrity as he had embraced it and proclaimed his reconversion to Sikhism. He tried to come to India but was turned back at Aden. The experience made him more bitter and he began to describe himself as the 'implacable foe of the British'. He tried to win the support of the French Government, the Tsar, the Kaiser and other European rulers; he set up an émigré one-man government and appointed one of the Sandhawalias to be his Chief Minister. He threatened to mount an invasion of India through the North-West frontier. Neither in the Punjab nor elsewhere in India did any one take Dalip Singh seriously. The bout of megalomania lasted a few years. On being assured that his debts would be cleared, he made an abject apology to the Queen for his past conduct, and resumed his profligate living. On the death of his Ethiopian wife, he married a French woman. He died on 23rd October 1893 in a hotel in Paris.

Dalip's mother, Jindan, had been exiled in July 1848. Her stipend was successively reduced from Rs. 1½ lakhs to to Rs. 48,000 and finally to Rs. 12,000 per year. She was stripped of all her private jewellery before she was sent to Benares. On 18th April 1849, she eluded the Security Police and escaped to Kathmandu. She probably expected a popular rising against the British or hoped that the Gurkhas would help her liberate the Punjab. Disappointed in her expectations, she left her refuge and in 1861 was allowed to rejoin her son in England. She set up an establishment of her own in Kensington, where she died two years later—a very sad and disappointed woman. Her last wish was: 'Do not let my bones rot in this inhospitable country. Take me back to India.' Her son brought her ashes to Hardwar to be scattered in the Ganges.

Dewan Mulraj was arrested and brought to Lahore to be tried for the murders of Vans Agnew and Anderson. The trial was a legal farce as Lord Dalhousie had already made up his mind on the guilt of the Dewan. Three months before the hearing, Dalhousie wrote: 'I cannot hang him, but I will do what he will think a thousand times worse: I will send him across the sea, what they call "black water" and dread far more than death.' The court consisting of three Englishmen carried out his instructions. It found Mulraj guilty of being an accessory to the murder of the two officers and sentenced him to death. The sentence was commuted to transportation for life. As Dalhousie had foreseen, Mulraj was terrified of being taken across the '*kala pani*', and fell ill waiting for the boat at Calcutta. He asked to be taken to Benares to die. The request was conceded. The Dewan died on the way to the holy city, on 11th August 1851 at the age of thirty-six.

Godar Singh, the real perpetrator of the Multan murders, was convicted and hanged.

Kahan Singh Man, the man who was destined to take Mulraj's place as Governor of Multan, met an undeservedly sad end. After the murders of the English officers, he and his young son were arrested and locked up in the fort dungeon with fetters on their feet. The explosion of the powder magazine on 30th December 1848 not only destroyed most of the defending garrison but also brought down the ceiling of the prison-house. Some days after the British had taken over the fort, the rubble was cleared. Beneath the caved-in walls of the dungeon were found two skeletons: one of an adult, the other of a child. Both had iron fetters round their ankles.

Chattar Singh and Sher Singh Attariwala were treated as prisoners of war and after the new masters were firmly in the saddle, released on parole to live in retirement in their village of Attari. Despite their efforts to prevent it, the Attariwalas continued to be lionised by the masses. The President of the Punjab Board utilised a flimsy excuse to get rid of them. The Attariwalas had fed Brahmins in their village during a solar eclipse. This was construed as a breach of the terms of parole. The President had them rearrested and ordered their deportation. It was a clean sweep. Along with the Attariwalas, others like Lal Singh Moraria were also arrested. Both Chattar Singh and Sher Singh died in exile.

There were other characters in the epic struggle of whom little has been recorded in books of history. When the Attariwalas and their armies laid down their arms, many men resolved to continue the struggle for freedom. The most celebrated amongst them were Bhai Maharaj Singh, Colonel Rachpal Singh and Narain Singh. They went from village to village trying to rouse the peasantry not to give in to the foreigner. The British promised handsome rewards for their capture—alive or dead—but the people did not betray the leaders. Ultimately the police net closed round these brave men. Narain Singh was taken alive; Colonel Rachpal Singh was captured near Aligarh, but after he had been mortally wounded. On the night of 28th December 1849, Bhai Maharaj Singh on whose head there was a prize of Rs. 10,000 was taken with a band of twenty-one unarmed followers. When he was brought to Jullundur prison, the guards put their rifles on the ground and went down on their knees to bow to him. For many days people from neighbouring villages–Hindus, Muslims and Sikhs–came to Jullundur to worship the walls in which the Bhai was imprisoned. 'The Guru is no ordinary man,' wrote Mr. Vansittart, who had arrested him, 'he is to the natives what Jesus is to the most zealous of Christians.' The Government could not risk a public trial in India and decided to deport him to Singapore. For three years, the Bhai was kept in a solitary cell. He died on 5th July 1856.

The spot where Bhai Maharaj Singh was cremated is today marked by a small shrine. A big hospital has been built near it. At all hours of the day or night, groups of men and women–Chinese, Malays, Tamils and Punjabis–come to pay their homage by leaving offerings of money and flowers, by burning joss-sticks and lighting oil lamps. A legend has grown that the blessings of the Saint buried in the shrine ensures success on the operating table. None of them have ever heard of the name of Bhai Maharaj Singh. He is simply known as the *Baba Karni Wala*–the old man of miracles.

In the Punjab, the memories of the men who fought the battles of Ferozeshahr and Sabraon, Chillianwala and Gujerat were soon forgotten. In the Great Munity of 1857, only eight years after the annexation of their kingdom, the Punjabis helped their erstwhile conquerors to defeat their Hindustani compatriots. A new generation of Punjabis who disowned their past was born. Instead of having nostalgic regret over the passing of the last independent kingdom of India many were proud to be the foremost in loyalty to the British Crown; instead of boasting of their forefathers' achievements in hurling back foreign invaders, they were pleased to be known as 'The Sword arm of the British Empire'. Thus was the sponge of oblivion passed over the slate of history.

Index